How To Develop And Manage A Successful Condominium

by Adam Starchild

Books for Business
New York - Hong Kong

How to Develop and Manage a Successful Condominium

by
Adam Starchild

ISBN 0-89499-056-X

Books for Business
New York - Hong Kong
http://www.businessbooksinternational.com

Table of Contents

Introduction

The word "condominium", according to Webster,
means individual ownership of a unit (as an
apartment) in a multi-unit structure.

These multi-unit groups may contain residential or commercial buildings, or be a combination of the two, but all types have one thing
in common. Any member of any condominium can sell,
mortgage or otherwise dispose of any unit. It is
the sole property of the purchaser, although it is
a part of a larger project.

Although the condominium concept burst upon
the American scene less than 20 years ago--an out-
growth of the price of urban real estate and housing
costs--it has an ancient tradition.

When all roads led to Rome, the automobile
was 2,000 years in the future. People whose interests

INTRODUCTION

lay in the political and economic spheres of the
far-flung empire had to stay close to the action.
They couldn't move to the suburbs and commute. As
a result, the Roman Senate passed the first condominium laws. In the Middle Ages, when people had to
stay within walled cities for protection, many lived
in condominiums. When civilization tamed the out-
lands the walled cities became, primarily, market
places, and most of the population bought cheaper
land adjacent to the town.

The condominium idea lay dormant from then
until the early 1900's when, first in the crowded
cities of Europe and later in the Western Hemisphere,
the costs of building and maintenance in the centers
of commerce caused it to bloom again. It put forth
new growth first in the inner city. This rapidly
spread to suburbia and even further--into vacation
homes, commercial ventures and retirement communi-
ties.

People who want housing or office space with
minimum maintenance costs, and developers who must
show a percentage of qualified tenants in order to
arrange financing for large projects both find the
flexibility of condominium construction equal to
their needs.

It may be that there is, indeed, nothing new
under the sun. But space-age technology and know-
how married to a concept from ancient Rome brought

forth a child for our time. The 20th century condominium.

The following chapters will show prospective developers and owners how to avoid pitfalls and be able to recognize a safe investment from a shaky one.

I. Advantages Stimulate Growth

I. Advantages Stimulate Growth

The principal advantage leading to the rapid
growth of condominiums is flexibility. The individual needs of different groups of people can
be brought under one roof, depending on the
development plan.

Residential condominiums can include: a
community of attached or detached one-family
houses; low-rise apartments, sometimes called
garden apartments; a group of one or more high-
rise buildings, or any combination of these.
Business condominiums usually house medical offices, shopping centers or other commercial services. Some projects contain both residential and
business property.

Whatever the arrangement, each condominium
member has a deed and title to each unit bought
and can vote on comdominium business in relation

to the size of the unit or units owned. Each unit
can be mortgaged by the owner and each is taxed
separately. No owner is liable for mortgage payments or taxes on other units, but is responsible
to the condominium association for the amount
allotted for common facilities.

Some of the advantages are easy to see. Since
condominiums are non-profit organizations, members
pay only their assessment of actual operating costs
There is no danger of escalating rents, which can
be the case when a landlord might take advantage
of an increased demand for rentals to add to profits. Mortgage interest and real estate taxes
can be deducted from income taxes, another bonus
not shared by renters. This arrangement gives the
condominium owner, whether residential or commercial, the same tax break as the holder of private
real estate.

One of the bases of the condominium concept
is that owners are usually more careful with property than renters, which works to cut the maintenance budget of the project. It is to the best
advantage of every owner to keep his unit in shape
and pay his share of the general maintenance and
improvements so that the resale equity will remain
high.

Another advantage accrues in the case where
the project has both commercial and residential

units. If commercial space is owned by the condominium association, it can be leased or rented to
a business, or the association can start a business
in such an area. Income from lease or rental of
commercial units can pay for some of the maintenance
charges which would ordinarily be the responsibility
of the individual owners.

Those who own vacation and second-home condominiums have still another advantage. They can
lease the units during the time they don't occupy
them and use the money for mortgage and maintenance
payments.

Condominiums are now an integral and growing
part of the construction scene, both for housing
and business. However, there are still risks to
both buyer and developer if a condominium is not
properly organized and based firmly on existing
statutes.

II. Differences Between A Condominium And A Cooperative

II. Differences Between A Condominium And A Cooperative

The words "condominium" and "cooperative" are often used interchangeably, but there are important differences.

In cooperative housing the members buy stock in a corporation, which leases apartments equivalent to the value of stock owned. The member leases his apartment only. He does not own it. He may sell it only to another person who can buy his amount of stock in the corporation. In contrast to this, the condominium buyer can pay cash and own his apartment outright, or finance his purchase through a mortgage, since a condominium unit is considered a piece of real estate separate from the common elements.

Taxes are figured as a percentage of the whole in a cooperative development. If a cooperative is less than 80% filled by residential units (for

17

example, if it's half residential and half commercial) the apartment leaser gets no tax break at
all. If it's more than 80% residential, he can
allow his share of taxes as an income tax deduction. The condominium owner is taxed only on his
unit, no matter how the rest of the building is
divided, because he has his own deed, and will always be able to deduct these expenses. The same
is true for interest on his mortgage.

In a cooperative each tenant pays a stated
amount to the corporate management to cover taxes,
amortization of the mortgage, interest and maintenance charges. If, for any reason, a number of
apartments become vacant, other owners have to pay
larger assessments for operating expense. His
security is based on what others may neglect.
Since, in a condominium, the areas of common contribution are much smaller, being limited to the
jointly-owned elements, risks are also less.

Some consider it an advantage that, since the
corporation owns all the property in a cooperative,
'it and it alone is responsible for mortgage payments
Further, it can finance major rehabilitation and
repairs with new mortgage money because it can
mortgage all the property, both common elements
and individual units, as one package. The
condominium format proscribes mortgaging the common
areas and the rest is divided into separate units,
so this type of financing for major repairs isn't

18

possible. However, if adequate reserve and
contingency funds are set aside by management,
which is necessary under FHA insured loans,
condominiums are prepared for major rehabilitation
without refinancing.

Flexibility of resale is another major
difference. The condominium owner, not hampered
by having to wait until someone can come up with
a considerable amount of money to buy stock in a
corporation, may dispose of his property under any
of the options given owners of single-family homes
He may also, if necessary, refinance his own unit,
which isn't possible in a cooperative.

Both types of development restrict, to some
extent, changes in interior design. Greater
flexibility in this area is allowed condominium
owners; however. Because of their direct ownership and responsibility for their own property,
they can adopt any style of decoration they want,
provided it doesn't change any of the structural
elements or interfere with the central areas.

Some people will prefer one type over the
other, depending on individual needs. They both
have advantages; however, the advantages are
slightly different in each case. And this is why
the words aren't really interchangeable.

A handy chart of the main differences will be
found on the following page.

DIFFERENCES BETWEEN A CONDO & A CO-OP

	COOPERATIVES	CONDOMINIUM
Mortgagor	The cooperative corporation	Each individual owner that borrowed money to purchase the unit
Mortgagee	The lending institution	Same
Monthly Charge	Proportionate share of all costs including mortgage	Percentage of common estate costs. Any mortgage payments on the individually owned unit are paid separately as those assessed on the individual unit.
Real Estate Taxes	Assessed on the property of the cooperative corporation	Assessed on the individual unit
Voting	Each member has one vote	Each owner has the number of votes representing the percentage of value of his unit to the total of all units.
Mortgage Term	Cooperative corporation usually has 40 years-- member is not a mortgagor.	Owner usually has 30 years--condominium is not a mortgagor.
Closing or Settlement costs	Costs in addition to the corporate property including mortgage service charge, title search, insurance and transfer of ownership charges paid when the cooperative first	Costs in addition to the price of a unit and its undivided interest in the common estate including mortgage service charge, title search, insurance and transfer of ownership charges paid each time the unit is resold or re-

	COOPERATIVES	CONDOMINIUM
	purchases the property. Only a small transfer fee is charged to transfer future membership in the cooperative.	financed.
Equity	Increase in the value of a membership certificate over and above the initial or "down payment" resulting from members monthly contribution toward payment of the corporate mortgage.	Increase in the value of ownership interest in the unit as the owner pays off his mortgage and from market value appreciation.
Escrow Funds	Subscription or down payments required to be held unused until the viable cooperative is assured. Tranfer of membership funds is sometimes escrowed until the transfer is completed.	Subscription or down payments required to be held unused until the condominium regime is recorded on the property and titles are conveyed to each buyer. Escrows are usually used in each resale situation. The deed is held in escrow until all conditions of the sale (including any prepayments) have been met.

III. Pre-Development

III. Pre-Development

Sound pre-development will often mean the difference between having a successful condominium or one which is hard to fill.

If it is done thoroughly it will be a firm foundation from which to launch a successful develop ment, but if many of the details are left until later, the builders, lenders and finally, prospective buyers will look for another investment for their time and money.

Demographics, the name of the game in politics and television advertising, is a good place to start. What age groups will find this development attrac- tive? What is their median income and how do they spend it? What is their life style? By asking these questions first, a developer can make sure his project is needed and marketable.

A newspaper ad about the type of condominium

to be offered should bring enough replies to tell
what the possible market is likely to be.

Location is the most important part of the
physical plan. A developer must think like the
buyers he's trying to reach when selecting the site.
It must be near shopping areas and recreation in
the case of a condominium for people who are retired
or nearing retirement age. For younger couples
and families, access to schools, highways and employment is important.

If possible, it's preferable to choose property away from airline and traffic patterns with
their attendant noise.

The price should be established before
contacting any prospective buyers. It must be
competitive with apartment rentals and single
family homes in the same neighborhood and offer a
comparable amount of living space and privacy. A
rule of thumb, except for luxury units, is that the
unit price should be a little more than rental
units, but a few percentage points less than the
cost for a private dwelling in the same area.

Sales prices are usually grouped into three
categories: moderate, better and best. A per-
square-foot cost is put on each type. These are
judged by factors such as access, view, location
within the building and size of the unit.

The potential developer must also check the neighborhood with a buyer's eye when it comes to resale value. If it is improving--new houses being built or the possibility of a new or expanded shopping center or school--resale value will be assured. The prospective buyer will consider this as a favorable point. It will also increase his trust in the developer and the project.

Good pre-planning includes a check of zoning regulations and other developments on the drawing board near the selected location. Other types of construction might alter, for better or worse, the values in the area.

The architect's plans should be available for inspection by the time the first buyers are contacted. If possible, a scale model incorporating the common areas, landscaping, unit sizes, and the outer design of the buildings is even better. Some condominiums in choice locations, developed for very special groups, have sold well without these tools of the trade, but it's not recommended.

FHA procedures allow the developer to determine whether or not people will be interested in a project without their binding themselves to the purchase of a unit, during the pre-development stage. The developer may ask a minimal fee (usually $50) from a potential buyer as evidence of interest, but can't accept a down payment until the FHA has reviewed and approved the proposal. This includes a commitment to insure mortgages on the project.

Under most state and federal regulations, this money is deposited in an escrow account. If the project doesn't materialize within a stated time, the money must be refunded. If the development is completed, the amounts collected are applied to the down payment.

Working within this set of rules, the developer can test the market without leaving the buyer unprotected.

Some states have established regulatory agencies to oversee condominium construction. Developers must answer a lengthy questionnaire before being allowed to make any public offering of sale.

If the pre-development work is done carefully, and in detail, the rest of the project will fall into place. Before seeking any buyers, a developer should ask himself every possible thing a buyer or his attorney might ask about the proposal and be able to give an adequate answer. This goes double for the questions which will be raised by the agencies and business interests that have to be approached for approval or financial backing. It would pay to retain a knowledgeable attorney and have him play devil's advocate, i.e. the role of a hard-nosed lawyer asking every conceivable question about the project in behalf of his fictional client. The tougher and more specific he is, the better for you.

The developer who has built and sold a number of successful condominiums was once a pre-developer who did his homework.

IV. Enabling Legislation

IV. Enabling Legislation

In the 1920's Brazil passed the first enabling
legislation in the Western Hemisphere for establishing the formation of condominiums. Chile followed
suit in 1937, and other Latin American countries
adopted laws for this type of housing in the next
two decades. A few organizations experimented
with condominiums in the United States in the late
1940's, but their efforts were short-lived.

In 1951 the Territory of Puerto Rico pioneered
the original legislation which became the basis of
later statutes in the United States. The Horizontal
Property Act of 1958 clarified the legal guidelines
for condominium development by stating the rules of
property ownership in such projects.

Interest in the United States still lagged
until 1961 when Congress added Section 234 to the
National Housing Act. This law provided that the

LEGISLATION

Federal Housing Administration could insure mortgages on condominiums. Although FHA doesn't lend money, it insures loans by private institutions to builders who meet certain standards. Most mortgages are not insured by FHA but private lenders use the government standards as a guide.

The financial institutions and buyers decided that if condominium loans were insurable by FHA, which later established guidelines similar to the Puerto Rican laws, they were safe to construct or purchase. Within six years, every state had enacted a condominium statute.

Although laws vary from state to state and the interpretation of these laws varies from community to community, the public decided that condominiums were here to stay.

U.S. STATUTES

Sponsors of legislation to establish the legality of condominiums in the separate states used the FHA Model Statute for Apartment Ownership (a copy of which is provided at the end of this chapter) as a guide.

In order to make the new laws effective, sponsors had to examine all the existing codes regarding taxation, real property, mortgages, sub-division platting. and zoning regulations: the

whole package of interlocking regulations that
constitutes the body of real estate statutes. Then
they had to pass legislation which would not conflict,
but would dove-tail with the acknowledged codes.

What they came up with was legislation called
the Apartment Ownership Acts of the separate states.
They differ in minor respects--in some states the
title is Horizontal Property Act--but all of them
insure the main points: namely, that a person may
own an individual apartment and at the same time
participate in ownership of common areas and facilities shared with others.

Readers will probably want to familiarize
themselves with the Model Act in its entirety, if
they are prospective condominium developers. To
give some idea of the main points, a brief summary
of the separate sections of the Act follows:

Sections 1 and 2 concern the title of the Act
and define all the terms used in its separate parts.
The definitions include what is meant by apartment,
common property, common profits, common expenses,
the Association of Apartment Owners and Declaration
within the framework of condominium legislation.

Section 3 states that the law applies to all
property mentioned in Section 2 and to all owners
of such property.

LEGISLATION

Sections 4 and 5 establish that the apartments are real property and deal with the individual ownership and possession.

Section 6 concerns the common property and the basic rules governing its use and maintenance. The state statutes differ on the leeway given apportionment of the undivided interest of each owner, but they are all agreed that it must remain undivided. The legalization of an apartment as real property which can be individually owned and the provisions establishing certain undivided property areas are the twin bases upon which the condominium concept rests.

Section 7 defines the responsibility of the owners with regard to the By-Laws.

Section 8 states the limits to be put on work engaged in by individual owners which might be dangerous to other owners and to the property as a whole.

Section 9 is a lengthy, but important explanation of the regulations concerning liens, both before and after individual units are sold. The limited liability for liens against the property of each owner and satisfaction by payment of the pro rata share of each unit is spelled out. This section was included to alleviate hardship and achieve the equitable treatment of all owners.

Section 10 outlines the division of common profits.

Section 11 concerns the Declaration, which must describe completely the land, buildings, number of apartments and how they may be identified; descriptions of both common interest and limited interest areas and facilities; and other details in regard to the value, purposes, restrictions, voting rights and methods for amending the Declaration. (The next chapter deals with the Declaration.)

Section 12 goes into what shall be included in the deeds to the separate apartments. This includes the dimensions of the unit, apartment number, a statement of its use and restrictions, and the percentage of undivided interest in the common areas allowable to each unit.

Section 13 states that a complete floor plan must be filed.

Section 14 gives the provisions covering the developer's blanket mortgage and how it should be dealt with when the apartments become individually owned. This section specifically mentions FHA regulations, which might not apply in some cases, such as with conventional condominiums not built with FHA standards. In these cases, the provisions may be deleted or others added, as necessary.

LEGISLATION

Section 15 deals with the recording of the Declaration and other papers which must be registered.

Section 16 and 17 concern the removal of individually held property which becomes part of the common interest and how the property may be resubmitted under individual ownership.

Section 18 and 19 deal with the contents of the By-Laws and their modification.

Section 20 states the rules for records of expenditures on the common property.

Section 21 declares that abandonment of an apartment or non-use of facilities does not exempt an owner from his share of the upkeep expense.

Section 22 defines the apartments as individually owned for tax purposes.

Section 23 makes liens for unpaid Association assessments subordinate to taxes and first mortgages of record to protect the first mortgagees. This protects the Association by giving it rights comparable to those of a second mortgagee. Although a first mortgagee may void liens against any one unit by foreclosure, the financial stability of the condominium is reasonably assured by

the provision that unpaid assessments against a
unit after foreclosure may be pro rated against
all owners, including the owner who obtains title
by foreclosure.

Section 24 concerns the liability of both
buyers and sellers of apartments toward the common
expenses.

Section 25: The FHA code did not cover insurance, except to state that it was the responsibility of the mortgagor. Insurance provisions,
however, are covered in Chapter 5. They are
included in the Enabling Declaration at the end
of that section.

Section 26 provides for the rights of individual
owners in the event of damage to the common property.
If common interests are sold, the owners divide the
funds according to their percentages.

Section 27 sets out the responsibilities and
rights of the Board of Directors regarding actions
to be brought against apartment owners.

Section 28 states that not only owners, but
tenants of the owners and employees are subject
to the provisions of the Act and the By-Laws of
the Association.

* * * *

LEGISLATION

Prospective developers and their legal advisors should make a careful study of the Model and compare it with the laws passed by the state in which they do business. Some states require more and others less than the suggested code. For example, in some places commercial condominiums are not allowed. In others, they're allowed but must not be mixed with residential units. Since each state has its own ground rules, developers familiar with what is possible in, say, Florida, might not find the same to be true in California or New York.

However, the basic rules as to what does and does not constitute a condominium apply everywhere and a thorough knowledge of the Model statute will always be necessary.

MODEL STATUTE FOR CREATION OF APARTMENT OWNERSHIP

Section 1: Apartment Ownership Act. This Act shall be known as the "Apartment Ownership Act".

Section 2: Definitions. As used in this Act, unless the context otherwise requires:

(a) "Apartment" means a part of the property intended for any type of independent use, including one or more rooms or enclosed spaces located on one or more floors (or part or parts thereof) in a building, and with a direct exit to a public street or highway or to a common area leading to such street or highway.

(b) "Apartment owner" means the person or persons owning an apartment in fee simple absolute and an undivided interest in the fee simple estate of the common areas and facilities in the percentage specified and established in the Declaration.

(c) "Apartment number" means the number, letter, or combination thereof, designating the apartment in the Declaration.

(d) "Association of apartment owners" means all of the apartment owners acting as a group in accordance with the By-Laws and Declaration.

(e) "Building" means a building, containing five or more apartments, with a total of five or more apartments for all such buildings, and comprising a part of the property. [Recommended definition conforms with the current FHA minimum eligibility requirements. Definition may be broadened to meet conventional condominium needs. Ed.]

(f) "Common areas and facilities," unless otherwise provided in the Declaration or lawful amendments thereto, means and includes:

    (1) The land on which the building is located;
    (2) The foundations, columns, girders, beams, supports, main walls, roofs, halls, corridors, lobbies, stairs, stairways, fire escapes, and entrances and exits of the building;
    (3) The basements, yards, gardens, parking areas and storage spaces;

(4) The premises for the lodging of janitors
or persons in charge of the property;

(5) Installations of central services such
as power, light, gas, hot and cold
water, heating, refrigeration, air
conditioning and incinerating;

(6) The elevators, tanks, pumps, fans,
compressors, ducts and in general all
apparatus and installations existing
for common use;

(7) Such community and commercial facilities
as may be provided for in the Declaration;
and

(8) All other parts of the property necessary or convenient to its existence,
maintenance and safety, or normally in
common use.

(g) "Common expenses" means and include:

(1) All sums lawfully assessed against the
apartment owners by the Association of
Apartment Owners;

(2) Expenses of administration, maintenance,
repair or replacement of the common
areas and facilities;

(3) Expenses agreed upon as common expenses
by the Association of Apartment Owners;

(4) Expenses declared common expenses by
provisions of this Act, or by the
Declaration or the By-Laws.

(h) "Common profits" means the balance of all
income, rents, profits and revenues from the common
areas and facilities remaining after the deduction
of the common expenses.

(i) "Declaration" means the instrument by which
the property is submitted to the provisions of this
Act, as hereinafter provided, and such Declaration
as from time to time may be lawfully amended.

(j) "Limited common areas and facilities" mean
and include those common areas and facilities designated in the Declaration as reserved for use of
certain apartment or apartments to the exclusion of
the other apartments.

(k) "Majority" or "Majority of apartment owners"
means the apartment owners with 51% or more of the
votes in accordance with the percentages assigned in

the Declaration to the apartments for voting purposes.

    (l) "Person" means individual, corporation
partnership, association, trustee or other legal
entity.

    (m) "Property" means and includes the land, the
building, all improvements and structures thereon,
all owned in fee simple absolute and all easements,
rights and appurtenances belonging thereto, and all
articles of personal property intended for use in
connection therewith, which have been or are intended
to be submitted to the provisions of this Act.

Section 3: Application of Act. This Act shall be
applicable only to property, the sole owner or all
of the owners of which submit the same to the provisions hereof by duly executing and recording a
Declaration as hereinafter provided.

Section 4: Status of the Apartments. Each apartment, together with its undivided interest in the
common areas and facilities, shall for all purposes
constitute real property.

Section 5: Ownership of Apartments. Each apartment owner shall be entitled to the exclusive
ownership and possession of his apartment.

Section 6: Common Areas and Facilities.

    (a) Each apartment owner shall be entitled to
an undivided interest in the common areas and
facilities in the percentage expressed in the
Declaration. Such percentage shall be computed by
taking as a basis the value of the apartment in
relation to the value of the property.

    (b) The percentage of the undivided interest
of each apartment owner in the common areas and
facilities as expressed in the Declaration shall
have a permanent character and shall not be altered
without the consent of all of the apartment owners
expressed in an amended Declaration duly recorded.
The percentage of the undivided interest in the
common areas and facilities shall not be separated
from the apartment to which it appertains and shall

be deemed to be conveyed or encumbered with the
apartment even though such interest is not
expressly mentioned or described in the conveyance
or other instrument.

(c) The common areas and facilities shall
remain undivided and no apartment owner or any
other person shall bring any action for partition
or division of any part thereof, unless the property
has been removed from the provisions of this Act
as provided in Section 16 and 26. Any covenant to
the contrary shall be null and void.

(d) Each apartment owner may use the common
areas and facilities in accordance with the purpose
for which they were intended without hindering or
encroaching upon the lawful rights of the other
apartment owners.

(e) The necessary work of maintenance, repair
and replacement of the common areas and facilities
and the making of any additions or improvements
thereto shall be carried out only as provided herein
and in the By-Laws.

(f) The Association of Apartment Owners shall
have the irrevocable right, to be exercised by the
manager or Board of Directors, to have access to
each apartment from time to time during reasonable
hours as may be necessary for the maintenance,
repair or replacement of any of the common areas
and facilities therein or accessible therefrom, or
for making emergency repairs therein necessary to
prevent damage to the common areas and facilities
or to another apartment or apartments.

Section 7: Compliance with Covenants, By-Laws and
Administrative Provisions. Each apartment owner
shall comply strictly with the By-Laws and with
the administrative rules and regulations adopted
pursuant thereto, as either of the same may be
lawfully amended from time to time, and with the
covenants, conditions and restrictions set forth
in the Declaration or in the deed to his apartment.
Failure to comply with any of the same shall be
ground for an action to recover sums due, for
damages or injunctive relief or both maintainable
by the manager or Board of Directors on behalf of
the Association of Apartment Owners or, in a proper

case, by an aggrieved apartment owner.

Section 8: Certain Work Prohibited. No apartment
owner shall do any work which would jeopardize the
soundness or safety of the property, reduce the
value thereof or impair any easement or hereditament
without in every such case the unanimous consent of
all the other apartment owners being first obtained.

Section 9: Liens Against Apartments; Removal from
Lien; Effect of Part Payment.

(a) Subsequent to recording the Declaration
as provided in this Act, and while the property
remains subject to this Act, no lien shall thereafter arise or be effective against the property.
During such period liens or encumbrances shall arise
or be created only against each apartment and the
percentage of undivided interest in the common
areas and facilities, appurtenant to such apartment,
in the same manner and under the same conditions in
every respect as liens or encumbrances may arise or
be created upon or against any other separate parcel
of real property subject to individual ownership;
provided that no labor performed or materials
furnished with the consent or at the request of an
apartment owner or his agent or his contractor or
subcontractor, shall be the basis for the filing
of a lien pursuant to the Lien Law against the
apartment or any other property of any other apartment owner not expressly consenting to or requesting
the same, except that such express consent shall be
deemed to be given by the owner of any apartment in
the case of emergency repairs thereto. Labor performed or materials furnished for the common areas
and facilities, if duly authorized by the Association
of Apartment Owners, the manager or Board of Directors
in accordance with this Act, the Declaration or By-
Laws, shall be deemed to be performed or furnished
with the express consent of each apartment owner
and shall be the basis for the filing of a lien
pursuant to the Lien Law against each of the apartments and shall be subject to the provisions of
subparagraph (b) hereunder.

(b) In the event a lien against two or more apartments becomes effective, the apartment owners of the separate apartments may remove their apartment and the percentage of undivided interest in the common areas and facilities appurtenant to such apartment from the lien by payment of the fractional or proportional amounts attributable to each of the apartments affected. Such individual payment shall be computed by reference to the percentages appearing on the Declaration. Subsequent to any such payment, discharge or other satisfaction the apartment and the percentage of undivided interest in the common areas and facilities appurtenant thereto shall thereafter be free and clear of the lien so paid, satisfied or discharged. Such partial payment, satisfaction or discharge shall not prevent the lienor from proceeding to enforce his rights against any apartment and the percentage of undivided interest in the common areas and facilities appurtenant thereto not so paid, satisfied or discharged.

Section 10: Common Profits and Expenses. The common profits of the property shall be distributed among, and the common expenses shall be charged to, the apartment owners according to the percentage of the undivided interest in the common areas and facilities.

Section 11: Contents of Declaration. The Declaration shall contain the following particulars:

1. Description of the land on which the building and improvements are or are to be located.
2. Description of the building, stating the number of stories and basements, the number of apartments and the principal materials of which it is or is to be constructed.
3. The apartment number of each apartment, and a statement of its location, approximate area, number of rooms, and immediate common area to which it has access, and any other data necessary for its proper identification.
4. Description of the common areas and facilities
5. Description of the limited common areas and

facilities, if any, stating to which apartments their use is reserved.

6. Value of the property and of each apartment, and the percentage of undivided interest in the common areas and facilities appertaining to each apartment and its owner for all purposes, including voting.

7. Statement of the purposes for which the building and each of the apartments are intended and restricted as to use.

8. The name of a person to receive service of process in the case hereinafter provided, together with the residence or place of business of such person which shall be within the city or county in which the building is located.

9. Provision as to the percentage of votes by the apartment owners which shall be determinative of whether to rebuild, repair, restore, or sell the property in the event of damage or destruction of all or part of the property.

10. Any further details in connection with the property which the person executing the Declaration may deem desirable to set forth consistent with this Act.

11. The method by which the Declaration may be amended, consistent with the provisions of this Act.

Section 12: Contents of Deeds of Apartments. Deeds of apartments shall include the following particulars

1. Description of the land as provided in Section 11 of this Act, or the post office address of the property, including in either case the liber, page and date of recording of the Declaration.

2. The apartment number of the apartment in the Declaration and any other data necessary for its proper identification.

3. Statement of the use for which the apartment is intended and restrictions on its use.

4. The percentage of undivided interest appertaining to the apartment in the common areas

and facilities.
5. Any further details which the grantor and grantee may deem desirable to set forth consistent with the Declaration and this Act.

Section 13: Copy of the Floor Plans to be Filed.
Simultaneously with the recording of the Declaration there shall be filed in the office of the recording officer a set of the floor plans of the building showing the layout, location, apartment numbers and dimensions of the apartments, stating the name of the building or that it has no name, and bearing the verified statement of a registered architect or licensed professional engineer certifying that it is an accurate copy of portions of the plans of the building as filed with and approved by the municipal or other governmental subdivision having jurisdiction over the issuance of permits for the construction of buildings. If such plans do not include a verified statement by such architect or engineer that such plans fully and accurately depict the layout, location, apartment numbers and dimensions of the apartments as built, there shall be recorded prior to the first conveyance of any apartment an amendment to the Declaration to which shall be attached a verified statement of a registered architect or licensed professional engineer certifying that the plans theretofore filed, or being filed simultaneously with such amendment, fully and accurately depict the layout, location, apartment numbers and dimensions of the apartments as built. Such plans shall be kept by the recording officer in a separate file for each building, indexed in the same manner as a conveyance entitled to record, numbered serially in the order of receipt, each designated "apartment ownership," with the name of the building, if any, and each containing a reference to the liber, page and date of recording of the Declaration. Correspondingly, the record of the Declaration shall contain a reference to the file number of the floor plans of the building affected thereby.

Section 14: Blanket Mortgages and Other Blanket Liens Affecting an Apartment at Time of First

Conveyance. At the time of the first conveyance of each apartment, every mortgage and other lien affecting such apartment, including the percentage of undivided interest of the apartment in the common areas and facilities, shall be paid and satisfied of record, or the apartment being conveyed and its percentage of undivided interest in the common areas and facilities shall be released there-from by partial release duly recorded. The suggested provision implements present FHA requirements con-concerning the removal of individual apartments from blanket mortgages. [The provision may be deleted, or other provisions added, to meet conventional condominium needs. Ed.]

Section 15: Recording.

(a) The Declaration, any amendment or amendments thereof, any instrument by which the provisions of this Act may be waived and every instrument affect-ing the property or any apartment shall be entitled to be recorded. Neither the Declaration nor any amendment thereof shall be valid unless duly re-corded.

(b) In addition to the records and indexes required to be maintained by the recording officer, the recording officer shall maintain an index or indexes whereby the record of each Declaration contains a reference to the record of each conveyance of an apartment affected by such Declaration, and the record of each conveyance of an apartment con-tains a reference to the Declaration of the building of which such apartment is a part.

Section 16: Removal From Provisions of This Act.

(a) All of the apartment owners may remove a property from the provisions of this Act by an instrument to that effect, duly recorded, provided that the holders of all liens affecting any of the apartments consent thereto or agree, in either case by instruments duly recorded, that their liens be transferred to the percentage of the undivided interest of the apartment owner in the property as hereinafter provided.

(b) Upon removal of the property from the provisions of this Act, the property shall be deemed to be owned in common by the apartment owners. The undivided interest in the property owned in common which shall appertain to each apartment owner shall be the percentage of undivided interest previously owned by such owner in the common areas and facilities.

Section 17: Removal No Bar to Subsequent Resubmission. The removal provided for in the preceding section shall in no way bar the subsequent resubmission of the property to the provisions of this Act.

Section 18: By-Laws. The administration of every property shall be governed by By-Laws, a true copy of which shall be annexed to the Declaration and made a part thereof. No modification of or amendment to the By-Laws shall be valid unless set forth in an amendment to the Declaration and such amendment is duly recorded.

Section 19: Contents of By-Laws. The By-Laws may provide for the following:

(a) The election from among the apartment owners of a Board of Directors, the number of persons constituting the same, and that the terms of at least one-third of the Directors shall expire annually; the powers and duties of the Board; the compensation, if any, of the Directors; the method of removal from office of Directors; and whether or not the Board may engage the services of a manager or managing agent.
(b) Method of calling meetings of the apartment owners; what percentage, if other than a majority of apartment owners shall constitute a quorum.
(c) Election of a President from among the Board of Directors who shall preside over the meetings of the Board of Directors and of the Association of Apartment Owners.
(d) Election of a Secretary who shall keep the minute book wherein resolutions shall be recorded.

(e) Election of a Treasurer who shall keep the financial records and books of account.

(f) Maintenance, repair and replacement of the common areas and facilities and payments therefor, including the method of approving payment vouchers.

(g) Manner of collecting from the apartment owners their share of the common expenses.

(h) Designation and removal of personnel necessary for the maintenance, repair and replacement of the common areas and facilities.

(i) Method of adopting and of amending administrative rules and regulations governing the details of the operation and use of the common areas and facilities.

(j) Such restrictions on and requirements respecting the use and maintenance of the apartments and the use of the common areas and facilities, not set forth in the Declaration, as are designed to prevent unreasonable interference with the use of their respective apartments and of the common areas and facilities by the several apartment owners.

(k) The percentage of votes required to amend the By-Laws.

(l) Other provisions as may be deemed necessary for the administration of the property consistent with this Act.

Section 20: Books of Receipts and Expenditures; Availability for Examination. The manager or Board of Directors, as the case may be, shall keep detailed, accurate records in chronological order, of the receipts and expenditures affecting the common areas and facilities, specifying and itemizing the maintenance and repair expenses of the common areas and facilities and any other expenses incurred. Such records and the vouchers authorizing the payments shall be available for examination by the apartment owners at convenient hours of week days.

Section 21: Waiver of Use of Common Areas and Facilities; Abandonment of Apartment. No apartment owner may exempt himself from liability for his contribution towards the common expenses by waiver of the use or enjoyment of any of the common areas and facilities or by abandonment of his apartment.

Section 22: Separate Taxation. Each apartment
and its percentage of undivided interest in the
common areas and facilities shall be deemed to be
a parcel and shall be subject to separate assessment and taxation by each assessing unit and
special district for all types of taxes authorized
by law including but not limited to special ad
valorem levies and special assessments. Neither
the building, the property nor any of the common
areas and facilities shall be deemed to be a parcel

Section 23: Priority of Lien.

(a) All sums assessed by the Association of
Apartment Owners but unpaid for the share of the
common expenses chargeable to any apartment shall
constitute a lien on such apartment prior to all
other liens except only (i) tax liens on the
apartment in favor of any assessing unit and
special district, and (ii) all sums unpaid on a
first mortgage of record. [Sponsors of legislation may wish to add to the list of liens which
will have priority over the assessments by the
Association of Apartment Owners. Ed.] Such lien
may be foreclosed by suit by the manager or Board
of Directors, acting on behalf of the apartment
owners, in like manner as a mortgage of real
property. In any such foreclosure the apartment
owner shall be required to pay a reasonable rental
for the apartment, if so provided in the By-Laws,
and the plaintiff in such foreclosure shall be entitled to the appointment of a receiver to collect
the same. The manager or Board of Directors,
acting on behalf of the apartment owners, shall
have power, unless prohibited by the Declaration,
to bid on the apartment at foreclosure sale, and
to acquire and hold, lease, mortgage and convey
the same. Suit to recover a money judgment for
unpaid common expenses shall be maintainable without foreclosing or waiving the lien securing the
same.
(b) Where the mortgagee of a first mortgage
of record or other purchaser of an apartment
obtains title to the apartment as a result of
foreclosure of the first mortgage, such acquirer

of title, his successors and assigns, shall not
be liable for the share of the common expenses or
assessments by the Association of Apartment Owners
chargeable to such apartment which became due
prior to the acquisition of title to such apartment by such acquirer. Such unpaid share of
common expenses or assessments shall be deemed to
be common expenses collectible from all of the
apartment owners including such acquirer, his
successors and assigns.

Section 24: Joint and Several Liability of Grantor
and Grantee for Unpaid Common Expenses. In a
voluntary conveyance the grantee of an apartment
shall be jointly and severally liable with the
grantor for all unpaid assessments against the
latter for his share of the common expenses up to
the time of the grant, or conveyance, without prejudice to the grantee's right to recover from the
grantor the amounts paid by the grantee therefor.
However, any such grantee shall be entitled to a
statement from the manager or Board of Directors,
as the case may be, setting forth the amount of
the unpaid assessments against the grantor and
such grantee shall not be liable for, nor shall the
apartment conveyed be subject to a lien for, any
unpaid assessments against the grantor in excess
of the amount therein set forth.

Section 25: Insurance. [Insurance was not discussed in the original statute because FHA
considered that insurance was the mortgagor's
responsibility. The right of the mortgagor to
obtain insurance was subsequently included in the
Enabling Declaration--See Chapter, Sections P & Q.]

Section 26: Disposition of Property; Destruction
or Damage. If, within _____ days of the date
of the damage or destruction to all or part of the
property, it is not determined by the Association
of Apartment Owners to repair, reconstruct or
rebuild, then and in that event:

(a) The property shall be deemed to be owned
in common by the apartment owners:

(b) The undivided interest in the property owned in common which shall appertain to each apartment owner shall be the percentage of undivided interest previously owned by such owner in the common areas and facilities;

(c) Any liens affecting any of the apartments shall be deemed to be transferred in accordance with the existing priorities to the percentage of the undivided interest of the apartment owner in the property as provided herein; and

(d) The property shall be subject to an action for partition at the suit of any apartment owner, in which event the net proceeds of sale, together with the net proceeds of the insurance on the property, if any, shall be considered as one fund and shall be divided among all the apartment owners in a percentage equal to the percentage of undivided interest owned by each owner in the property, after first paying out the respective shares of the apartment owners, to the extent sufficient for the purpose, all liens on the undivided interest in the property owned by each apartment owner.

Section 27: Actions. Without limiting the rights of any apartment owner, actions may be brought by the manager or Board of Directors, in either case in the discretion of the Board of Directors, on behalf of two or more of the apartment owners, as their respective interests may appear, with respect to any cause of action relating to the common areas and facilities or more than one apartment. Service of process on two or more apartment owners in any action relating to the common areas and facilities or more than one apartment may be made on the person designated in the Declaration to receive service of process.

Section 28: Personal Application.

(a) All apartment owners, tenants of such owners, employees of owners and tenants, or any other persons that may in any manner use property or any part thereof submitted to the provisions of this Act shall be subject to this Act and to the Declaration and By-Laws of the Association of

Apartment Owners adopted pursuant to the provisions
of this Act.

(b) All agreements, decisions and determinations lawfully made by the Association of
Apartment Owners in accordance with the voting
percentages established in the Act, Declaration
or By-Laws, shall be deemed to be binding on all
apartment owners.

Section 29: Severability. If any provision of
this Act or any section, sentence, clause, phrase
or word, or the application thereof in any cir-
cumstance is held invalid, the validity of the
remainder of the Act and of the application of
any such provision, section, sentence, clause,
phrase or word in any other circumstances shall
not be affected thereby.

V. Organizational Documents

V. Organizational Documents

Landmark federal and state legislation inevitably spawns new forms to be mastered and the FHA Code is no exception. The most important of these is the Declaration referred to in Section 11 of the Model statute.

Because of the dual nature of condominiums--some units owned separately, with common elements owned jointly--the legal basis had to be established to protect the interests of the developers and eventual owners as well as define the new type of property for tax purposes.

In order to spell out the nature of unit ownership and the right of the owner to transfer his property, with its entitlement to the common elements, new forms had to be worked out. The Enabling Declaration and the papers to be filed with it cover all areas where difficulties could arise under this new type of housing where individual ownership and joint ownership are indivisible, and the individual owner binds himself to assessments for upkeep of common property.

The form previously referred to as the Declaration or Enabling Declaration is also called the Master Deed, Matrix Deed or Deed of Constitution. These are all one and the same, depending on the language chosen by the lawmakers of the various State legislatures.

This Master Deed/Enabling Declaration, whichever it is called, is the instrument that commits the land to use as a condominium. A model Master Deed and a model Enabling Declaration are both included at the end of this chapter.

All discussion which follows applies to both, although for the sake of clarity we will use the designation Master Deed or Deed, since it is more familiar to most people.

The preamble states that the owners of a certain piece of property submit it as a condominium. This is followed by a complete description of the land, all buildings which are or will be constructed on it, and exact descriptions of the units within the buildings.

The Deed then designates the common elements

and the percentage of undivided interest in such facilities to which each owner is entitled.

In condominiums with different sized units these percentages may vary. In those with all units of approximately the same size the same percentage is used for each, i.e., 60 units: 1/60th interest. These percentages are also used for the establishment of the owner's share of upkeep and maintenance.

The purposes for which all parts of the condominium are to be used must also be thoroughly spelled out. This is necessary in all cases. Each area so designated will have to remain in that category for the life of the condominium, unless the Deed is amended. For example, in a project which is divided between residential and commercial use, the business sections will remain commercial and the residential units cannot be used for business.

If amendments become necessary for any reason, it should be specifically stated how the amendment can be made and by whom, and the percentages necessary to carry. In some projects it is 100 percent, but this is considered extreme. Most average between 51 and 75 percent.

Since the developer controls the Association

of Owners from the time the Master Deed is
recorded until the election of a Board of
Directors, the Deed must contain no language which
would permit the developer to enter any long-term
agreements, such as management contracts. This
is the prerogative of the permanent Board after
it is elected by the owners.

Another stipulation of the Master Deed is
that it must delegate the procedures under which
the owners will elect, and what powers they will
vest in the Board of Directors.

Many condominiums include the right of first
refusal to the Board, in the case of owners who
wish to sell. Such a right doesn't restrict the
amount of profit an owner can make on resale, but
it gives the other owners the option to buy the
unit at the best price offered.

Insurance provisions, both for commonly held
areas and those on private units, are required in
the Master Deed. The owner's assessment charge
covers expenses of insurance on the commonly held
property. If he wants further coverage on his
individual unit, it is handled as a private
transaction.

The Master Deed is the most important single
document to be filed because its accuracy as to

building dimensions and materials, and the pre-
sentation of other details, will depend on the
approval of the builder, lender, title insurance
company and recorder of deeds. And beyond this,
federal and/or state agencies will also use it as
a basis for granting the required permits and
licenses.

Developers may acquaint themselves with the
regulations regarding what should be included in
the Master Deed or Enabling Declaration by
studying the models which follow.

ORGANIZATIONAL DOCUMENTS

PLAN OF APARTMENT OWNERSHIP

MASTER DEED*

In the City of _____, County
of _____, and State of _____,
on this _____ day of _____, 19____,
_____, a corporation
organized and existing under the laws of the _____
_____ of _____, whose principal
office and domicile is situated in the City of _____
_____, State of _____, hereinafter
referred to as Grantor represented in this Deed
by its President, _____, who
is fully empowered and qualified to execute this
Deed on behalf of said corporation, does hereby
state:

FIRST: That Grantor owns the following
property situated in the City of _____,
State of _____, which is described as
follows:**

and recorded in the Office of the Recorder of the
County of _____, State of _____,
in Book _____ of Deeds at page_____.

SECOND: That Grantor has constructed on the
parcel of land described above a project known as
_____

*Form of deed should conform with statutory requirements
of jurisdiction where property is located. Enabling Declaration, FHA Form No. 3276-A, may be used in lieu of Master Deed
where local law permits.

**Insert metes and bounds description of land upon
which the project is constructed.

_____, according to
the plans attached hereto as Exhibit "A" which
were approved by the Planning Board of the City
of _____, State of _____,
on the _____ day of _____, 19_____,
and which are made a part hereof.

THIRD: That the said project consists of a
basement, a ground floor and _____ upper floors.
The ground floor will be used for commercial
facilities,* or other common purposes. The _____
_____ upper floors consist of individual apartments all for residential purposes. The _____
upper floors are all capable of individual utili-
zation on account of having their own exit to a
common area and facility of the project, and the
apartments will be sold to one or more owners,
each owner obtaining a particular and exclusive
property right thereto, hereinafter referred to
as "family unit", and also an undivided interest
in the general and/or restricted common areas
and facilities of the project, as listed hereinafter in this Deed, necessary for their adequate
use and enjoyment and hereinafter referred to as
"general and/or restricted common areas and facilities", all of the above in accordance with**

FOURTH: That the aforesaid project has a
total building area of _____ square feet, of
which _____ square feet, will constitute family
units, and _____ square feet will constitute
general and/or restricted common areas and facilities.

FIFTH: That the family units and common
areas and facilities of the project will be as

_____

*Approval for commercial facilities must be obtained
from FHA.

**Identify the state law establishing apartment ownership

65

follows:

1. Family Units - Upper Floors: In each of
the _____ upper floors there are _____ family
units. The said family units will be numbered
consecutively from one to _____ on each floor.
These numbers will be preceded by the tenth
which corresponds to each floor to wit: those
of the first floor will bear the numbers "101",
"102", et cetera; those of the second floor the
numbers "201", "202", et cetera; and those of
the higher floors will be numbered similarly
according to the corresponding tenth of each
floor. Hereinafter such family units will be
referred to as Family Unit Type Number One,
Family Unit Type Number Two, et cetera, respectively.

   Each family unit is equipped with*

   The family units are described hereinbelow.
The measure of the family unit include all of the
outside walls and one-half of the block partitions
but exclude bearing walls.

   (a) Family Unit Type Number One: It is a
rectangular shaped apartment measuring _____
feet long and _____ feet wide, making a total
area of _____ square feet, as specifically
shown in Exhibit A of this Deed. Its boundaries
are as follows:**

                              Its main door has access
to the corridor of the respective floor.

_____

   *Describe air conditioning units, if any, and other
equipment which is attached to or is a part of realty of
the family unit.

   **Conform boundary description to actual facts.

The family unit consists of the following rooms: a hall of _____ square feet, a living room of _____ square feet, a dining room of _____ square feet, a kitchen of _____ square feet, which includes the sinks, a _____ gas range, model _____ color _____; _____ bedrooms of _____ square feet, bathroom of _____ square feet. In addition, the family unit has a balcony facing _____ Street of _____ square feet.* (A description of each type of family unit should follow as items (b), (c), (d), etc.)

2. <u>Common Areas and Facilities</u>:

(a) The parcel of land described in Paragraph First of this Deed.

(b) A basement as shown in Exhibit A attached hereto and consisting of _____ square feet.

(c) The following facilities located in the basement:**

(d) Parking facilities as shown in Exhibit A attached hereto and consisting of _____ square feet.

(e) The ground floor as shown in Exhibit A attached and consisting of _____ square feet.

(f) The following facilities located in the ground floor:

    (1) Commercial areas and facilities as shown in Exhibit A attached hereto, consisting of _____ square feet and described as follows:***

    (2) A lobby and facilities as shown in Exhibit A attached hereto, consisting

---

*Conform description of rooms to actual facts. Material above is for guidance only.

**Describe in detail the items located in the basement

***Describe in detail commerical areas and facilities.

of _____ square feet, and
described as follows:*

(3) _____,**
   (g) The following facilities located
throughout the project and as shown in Exhibit A,
attached hereto:
   (1) _____ elevators.
   (2) An elevator shaft of _____ square
       feet, for the elevators extending
       from the ground floor up to the
       _____ floor.
   (3) A stairway, referred to in this
       Deed as stairway "A", of _____
       square feet, which leads from the
       ground floor to the roof of the
       project.
   (4) A stairway, referred to in this
       Deed as stairway "B", of _____
       square feet which leads from the
       open court to the _____ upper
       floor.
   (5) A flue extending from the incinerator
       in the basement to the roof of the
       project. The said flue will have a
       hopper door in each one of the _____
       _____ upper floors for the disposal
       of garbage and rubbish, and will be
       fed from the janitor's room of each
       of the _____ upper floors.
   (6) Water tank located on the roof of the
       project.
   (7) Elevator penthouse with corresponding
       elevator equipment located on the
       roof of the project.
   (8) Plumbing network throughout the
       project.
   (9) Electric and telephone wiring net-
       work throughout the project.
   (10) Necessary light, telephone and water
        public connections.

_____

*Describe in detail the lobby and its facilities.

**Include any other areas, rooms, etc. not mentioned above

(11) The foundations and main walls of
the project as described in the
plans which form part of this
Deed as Exhibit "A" hereof.*

(h) The following facilities located in each
one of the _____ upper floors and as shown
in Exhibit A, attached hereto, are restricted
common areas and facilities restricted to the
family units of each respective floor:

(1) A lobby which gives access to the
_____ elevators, to the
family unit, to the janitor's room,

to the corridor and to Stairway
"A".
(2) A room for the use of the janitor.
(3) A corridor extending from the lobby
to stairway "B".**

SIXTH:

(a) That the title and interest of each
owner of a family unit in the general common
areas and facilities listed under letters (a)
through (g) of subparagraph Two (2) of Paragraph
Fifth, and their proportionate share in the
profits and common expenses in the said general
common areas and facilities, as well as the
proportionate representation for voting purposes
in the meeting of the Association of Owners of
the _____ Condominium is based
on the proportionate value of all family units
as follows:

Family Unit Type Number One:

---

*Conform description of facilities located throughout
the building to actual facts. Material above is for
guidance only.

**Conform description of restricted common areas and
facilities to actual facts. Material above is for
guidance only.

_____ percent based on a value of
$_____ * for this apartment and a total value
of $_____ * for all family units. (Here follows
the proportionate value of Family Unit Type
Number Two through Family Unit Type Number
_____.)

_____ (b) That the title and interest of each owner
of the family units located on each of the _____
upper floors in the restricted common areas and
facilities located in the respective floor and
listed under letter (h) of said subparagraph Two
(2) of Paragraph Fifth, and their proportionate
share in the profits and common expenses in the
said restricted common areas and facilities, as
well as the proportionate representation for
voting purposes with respect to the said restricted
common areas and facilities in the meeting of the
Association of Owners of the _____
Condominium is based on the proportionate value
of each family unit to the total value of all
family units located on its respective floor, as
follows:

Family Unit Type Number One:

_____ percent

(Here follows the title and interest of the
family unit owners of Family Units Type Number
Two through Family Units Type Number _____,
in the restricted common areas and facilities
located in their respective floors.)

_____ (c) The proportionate representation for
voting purposes provided in (a) and (b) hereof
may be limited in accordance with the provisions
of the By-Laws attached hereto as Exhibit "B".

SEVENTH: That the administration of _____
_____ Condominium consisting as aforesaid
of the project and parcel of land described in
paragraphs "FIRST" and "FIFTH" of this Deed shall
be in accordance with the provisions of this Deed,

_____

*Value to correspond to FHA appraised value.

and with the provisions of the By-Laws which are made a part of this Deed and are attached hereto as Exhibit B, and shall be subject to the terms of a Regulatory Agreement executed by the Association of Owners and the Commissioner of the Federal Housing Administration which is made a part hereof and is attached as Exhibit C.

EIGHTH: That as appears above a plan of apartment ownership is hereby constituted under and subject to the provisions of*

so that the family units of the _____ upper floors may be conveyed and recorded as individual properties capable of independent use, on account of each having its own exit to a common area and facility of the project, each family unit owner having an exclusive and particular right over his respective family unit and in addition the specified undivided interest in the common areas and facilities and/or restricted common areas and facilities.

NINTH: That for the purpose of the recording fees to be imposed on the recordation of this Deed in the Book of Deeds, the value of the ___ _____ Condominium is distributed as follows:

(a) Parcel of land described in Paragraph "FIRST" hereof is valued at _____ Dollars.**
(b) The project described in Paragraphs "SECOND" and "THIRD" hereof is valued at _____ _____ Dollars.**

TENTH: That so long as the Grantor owns one or more of the family units, the Grantor shall be subject to the provision of the Deed and of the Exhibits "A", "B" and "C" attached hereto; and the Grantor covenants to take no action which

----

*Identify the state law establishing apartment ownership.

**Value to correspond to FHA appraised value.

will adversely affect the rights of the Association with respect to assurances against latent defects in the project or other rights assigned to the Association, the members of such association and their successors in interest, as their interest may appear, by reason of the establishment of the condominium.

ELEVENTH: That the general and/or restricted common areas and facilities shall remain undivided and no owner shall bring any action for partition or division.

TWELFTH: That the percentage of the undivided interest in the general and/or restricted common areas and facilities established herein shall not be changed except with the unanimous consent of all of the owners expressed in amendment to this Deed duly recorded.

THIRTEENTH: That the undivided interest in the general and/or restricted common areas and facilities shall not be separated from the unit to which it appertains and shall be deemed conveyed or encumbered with the unit even though such interest is not expressly mentioned or described in the conveyance or other instrument.

FOURTEENTH: That each owner shall comply with the provisions of this Deed, the By-Laws, decisions and resolutions of the Association of Owners or its representative, and the Regulatory Agreement, as lawfully amended from time to time, and failure to comply with any such provisions, decisions or resolutions, shall be grounds for an action to recover sums due, for damages, or for injunctive relief.

FIFTEENTH: That the dedication of the property to the Plan of Apartment Ownership herein shall not be revoked, or the property removed from the Plan of Apartment Ownership, or any of the provisions herein amended unless all of the owners and the mortgagees of all of the mortgages covering the units unanimously agree to such revocation,

or amendment, or removal of the property from the
Plan by duly recorded instruments.

SIXTEENTH: That no owner of a family unit
may exempt himself from liability for his contribution towards the common expenses by waiver of
the use or enjoyment of any of the general and/
or restricted common areas and facilities or by
the abandonment of his family unit.

SEVENTEENTH: That all present or future
owners, tenants, future tenants, or any other
person that might use the facilities of the
project in any manner, are subject to the provisions of this Deed and that the mere acquisition
or rental of any of the family units of the project or the mere act of occupancy of any of said
units shall signify that the provisions of this
Deed are accepted and ratified.

The respective "family units" shall not be
rented by the owners thereof for transient or
hotel purposes, which shall be defined as (a) rental
for any period less than thirty (30) days; or
(b) any rental if the occupants of the "family
unit" are provided customary hotel services, such
as room service for food and beverage, maid service, furnishing laundry and linen, and bellboy
service. Other than the foregoing obligations,
the owners of the respective "family units" shall
have the absolute right to lease same provided
that said lease is made subject to the covenants
and restrictions contained in this Declaration
and further subject to the By-Laws and Regulatory
Agreement attached hereto.

EIGHTEENTH: That if the property subject
to the Plan of Apartment Ownership is totally
or substantially damaged or destroyed, the
repair, reconstruction, or disposition of the
property shall be as provided by _____.*

_____

*Insert applicable statutory reference, or in the
absence of statute, insert the following "an agreement
approved by _____ of the votes."

NINETEENTH: That, where a mortgagee or other purchaser of a family unit obtains title by reason of foreclosure of a mortgage covering a unit, such acquirer of title, his successors or assigns, shall not be liable for assessments by the Association which became due prior to the acquisition of title by such acquirer, it being understood, however, that the above shall not be construed to prevent the Association from filing and claiming liens for such assessments and enforcing same as provided by law, and that such assessment liens shall be subordinate to such mortgage.*

TWENTIETH: That in a voluntary conveyance of a family unit the grantee of the unit shall be jointly and severally liable with the grantor for all unpaid assessments by the Association against the latter for his share of the common expenses up to the time of the grant or conveyance without prejudice to the grantee's right to recover from the grantor the amounts paid by the grantee therefor. However, any such grantee shall be entitled to a statement from the manager or Board of Directors of the Association, as the case may be, setting forth the amount of the unpaid assessments against the grantor due the Association and such grantee shall not be liable for, nor shall the family unit conveyed be subject to a lien for, any unpaid assessments made by the Association against the grantor in excess of the amount therein set forth.

TWENTY-FIRST: That the Board of Directors of the Association of Owners, or the Management Agent, or Manager shall obtain and continue in effect blanket property insurance in form and amounts satisfactory to mortgagees holding first mortgages covering family units but without pre-

---

*This provision is to be included in all Plans of Apartment Ownership where local law permits. Where more express provisions are required, items "J" and "K" of the "Enabling Declaration," FHA Form No. 3276-A may be used in lieu of this paragraph.

judice to the right of the owner of a family unit to obtain individual family unit insurance.

TWENTY-SECOND: That insurance premiums for any blanket insurance coverage shall be a common expense to be paid by monthly assessments levied by the Association of Owners; and that such payments shall be held in a separate escrow account of the Association of Owners and used solely for the payment of the blanket property insurance premiums as such premiums become due.

EXECUTION AND ACKNOWLEDGEMENT
AS REQUIRED BY STATE STATUTE

ORGANIZATIONAL DOCUMENTS

ENABLING DECLARATION

ESTABLISHING A PLAN FOR CONDOMINIUM OWNERSHIP

     WHEREAS, _____,
(hereinafter referred to as "Grantor") owns certain
real property herein described; and

     WHEREAS, said Grantor has improved said
property by constructing thereon a _____
unit multifamily structure known as _____
_____, said structure having been con-
structed in accordance with plans and specifications
prepared by _____, said plans being
on record in the _____, of the City
of _____, State of _____
and styled _____, FHA Project No. __
_____, and consisting of sheets _____
_____ through _____, through _____,
etc., all inclusive; and

     WHEREAS, said Grantor hereby establishes by
this declaration a plan for the individual ownership
of the real property estates consisting of the area
or space contained in each of the apartment units
in said multifamily structure, and the co-ownership
by the individual and separate owners thereof, as
tenants in common, of all of the remaining real
property which is hereinafter defined and referred
to herein as the "common areas and facilities".

     NOW, THEREFORE, said Grantor, the fee owner
of the following described real property, to-wit:

     (Land description)

hereby makes the following declaration as to
divisions, covenants, restrictions, limitations,
conditions and uses to which the above described
real property and improvements thereon, consisting

of a _____ unit multifamily structure of appurtenances, may be put, hereby specifying that said declaration shall constitute covenants to run with the land and shall be binding on said Grantor, its successors and assigns, and all subsequent owners of all or any part of said real property and improvements, together with their grantee, successors, heirs, executors, administrators, devisees or assigns:

A. Said Grantor, in order to establish a plan of condominium ownership for the above-described property and improvements, hereby covenants and agrees that it hereby divides said real property into the following separate freehold estates:

    1. The _____ separately designated and legally described freehold estates consisting of the spaces or areas, being the area or space contained in the perimeter walls of each of the _____ apartment units in said multifamily structure constructed on said property, said spaces being defined, and referred to herein, as "apartment spaces".

    2. A freehold estate consisting of the remaining portion of the real property is described and referred to herein as the "common areas and facilities", which definition includes the multifamily structure and the property upon which it is located, and specifically includes, but is not limited to, the land, roof, main walls, slabs, elevator, elevator shaft, staircases, lobbies, halls, parking spaces, storage spaces, community and commercial facilities, swimming pool, pumps, water tank, trees, pavement, balconies, pipes, wires, conduits, air conditioners and ducts, or other public utility lines.

B. For the purpose of this declaration, the ownership of each "apartment space" shall include the respective undivided interest in

the common areas and facilities specified and
established in "E" hereof, and each "apartment
space" together with the undivided interest is
defined and hereinafter referred to as "family
unit".

C. A portion of the "common areas and facilities"
is hereby set aside and allocated for the
restricted use of the respective "apartment
spaces", as is hereinafter designated, and as
shown on survey attached hereto, and said
areas shall be known as "restricted common
areas and facilities".

D. The _____ individual "apart
ment spaces" hereby established and which shall
be individually conveyed are described as
follows:

(Legal description of apartment spaces)

E. The undivided interest in the "common areas
and facilities" hereby established and which
shall be conveyed with each respective
"apartment space" is as follows:

(Apartment number - Percentage of undivided
interest)

The above respective undivided interests
established and to be conveyed with the
respective "apartment spaces" as indicated
above, cannot be changed, and said Grantor,
its successors and assigns, and grantees,
covenant and agree' that the undivided interests
in the "common areas and facilities" and the
fee titles to the respective "apartment spaces"
conveyed therewith, shall not be separated or
separately conveyed, and each said undivided
interest shall be deemed to be conveyed or

encumbered with its respective "apartment space even though the description in the instrument of conveyance or encumbrance may refer only to the fee title to the "apartment space".

F. The proportionate shares of the separate owners of the respective "family units" in the profits and common expenses in the "common areas and facilities", as well as their proportionate representation for voting purposes in the Association of Owners, is based on the proportionate value that each of the "family units", referred to herein, bears to the value of $ _____ ,* which represents the total value of all of the "family units". The value of the respective "family units", their respective interests for voting purposes, and their proportionate shares in the common profits and expenses shall be as follows:

(Family unit number - value* - Proportionate representation for voting and share in common profits and expenses)

G. The "restricted common areas and facilities" allocated for the restricted uses of the respective "family units" are as follows:

FAMILY UNIT 1: That portion of the parking area designated as parking space No. 1: storage space No. 1; together with balcony adjoining the "apartment space" associated with family unit 1 on the south. Said restricted areas are further described, located, and shown on survey attached hereto.**

H. That attached hereto and made a part hereof as Exhibit "A" is a survey consisting of ____

---

*Value to correspond with FHA appraised value.

**Descriptive material for guidance only; conform to actual facts.

_____ sheets as prepared by _____
_____, dated _____.

I. Said Grantor, its successors and assigns, by
this declaration, and all future owners of
the "family units", by their acceptance of
their deeds, covenant and agree as follows:

1. That the "common areas and facilities"
shall remain undivided, and no owner shall
bring any action for partition, it being
agreed that this restriction is necessary
in order to preserve the rights of the
owners with respect to the operation and
management of the condominium.

2. That the "apartment spaces" shall be
occupied and used by the respective
owners only as a private dwelling for
the owner, his family, tenants and social
guests and for no other purpose.

3. The owner of the respective "apartment
spaces" shall not be deemed to own the
undecorated and/or unfinished surfaces of
the perimeter walls, floors and ceilings
surrounding his respective "apartment
space", nor shall said owner be deemed to
own pipes, wires, conduits or other public
utility lines running through said respective "apartment spaces" which are utilized
for, or serve more than one "apartment
space", except as tenants in common with
the other "family unit" owners as hereto-
fore provided in "E". Said owner, however,
shall be deemed to own the walls and partitions which are contained in said owner's
respective "apartment space", and also shall
be deemed to own the inner decorated and/or
finished surfaces of the perimeter walls,
floors and ceilings, including plaster,
paint, wallpaper, etc.

4. The owners of the respective "apartment
spaces" agree that if any portion of the
"common areas and facilities" encroaches
upon the "apartment spaces", a valid
easement for the encroachment and for the

80

maintenance of same, so long as it stands, shall and does exist. In the event the multifamily structure is partially or totally destroyed, and then rebuilt, the owners of "apartment spaces" agree that minor encroachment of parts of the "common areas and facilities" due to construction shall be permitted and that valid easement for said encroachment and the maintenance thereof shall exist.

5. That an owner of a "family unit" shall automatically, upon becoming the owner of a "family unit or units", be a member of _____, hereinafter referred to as the "Association", and shall remain a member of said Association until such time as his ownership ceases for any reason, at which time his membership in said Association shall automatically cease.

6. That the owners of "family units" covenant and agree that the administration of the condominium shall be in accordance with the provisions of this Declaration, the By-Laws of the Association which are made a part hereof and attached as Exhibit "B", and shall be subject to the terms of a Regulatory Agreement executed by the Association and the Commissioner of the Federal Housing Administration, which Agreement is made a part hereof and is attached as Exhibit "C".

7. That each owner, tenant or occupant of a "family unit" shall comply with the provisions of this Declaration, the By-Laws, decisions and resolutions of the Association or its representative, and the Regulatory Agreement, as lawfully amended from time to time, and failure to comply with any such provisions, decisions, or resolutions, shall be grounds for an action to recover sums due, for damages, or for injunctive relief.

8. That this Declaration shall not be revoked or any of the provisions herein amended

81

unless all of the owners and the mortgagees of all of the mortgages covering the "family units" unanimously agree to such revocation or amendment by duly recorded instruments.

9. That no owner of a "family unit" may exempt himself from liability for his contribution towards the common expenses by waiver of the use or enjoyment of any of the common areas and facilities or by the abandonment of his "family unit".

J. All sums assessed by the Association but unpaid for the share of the common expenses chargeable to any family unit shall constitute a lien on such family unit prior to all other liens except only (1) tax liens on the family unit in favor of any assessing unit and special district, and (2) all sums unpaid on the first mortgage of record.* Such lien may be foreclosed by suit by the manager or Board of Directors, acting on behalf of the owners of the family units, in like manner as a mortgage of real property. In any such foreclosure the family unit owner shall be required to pay a reasonable rental for the family unit, if so provided in the By-Laws, and the plaintiff in such foreclosure action shall be entitled to the appointment of a receiver to collect the same. The manager or Board of Directors, acting on behalf of the owners of the family units, shall have power, unless prohibited herein, to bid on the unit at foreclosure sale, and to acquire and hold, lease, mortgage and convey the same. Suit to recover a money judgment for unpaid common expenses shall be maintainable without foreclosing or waiving the lien securing the same.

K. Where the mortgagee of a first mortgage of

---

*The list of liens having priority over the assessments by the Association for common expenses may be expanded provided the approval of FHA is obtained.

record or other purchaser of a family unit
obtains title to the unit as a result of
foreclosure of the first mortgage, such
acquirer of title, his successors and assigns,
shall not be liable for the share of the
common expenses or assessments by the Association chargeable to such family unit which became due prior to the acquisition of title
to such family unit by such acquirer. Such
unpaid share of common expenses or assessments
shall be deemed to be common expenses collectible from all of the family units including
such acquirer, his successors and assigns.

L. The respective "family units" shall not be
   rented by the owners thereof for transient
   or hotel purposes, which shall be defined as
   (a) rental for any period less than thirty
   (30) days; or (b) any rental if the occupants
   of the "family unit" are provided customary
   hotel services, such as room service for food
   and beverage, maid service, furnishing laundry
   and linen, and bellboy service. Other than
   the foregoing obligations, the owners of the
   respective "family units" shall have the
   absolute right to lease same provided that
   said lease is made subject to the covenants
   and restrictions contained in this Declaration
   and further subject to the By-Laws and Regulatory Agreement attached hereto.

M. In the event that the property subject to this
   Enabling Declaration is totally or substantially
   damaged or destroyed, the repair, reconstruction,
   or disposition of the property shall be as
   provided by _____.*

N. In a voluntary conveyance of a family unit the
   grantee of the unit shall be jointly and

_____

"Insert applicable statutory reference; or, in the
absence of statute, insert the following: "an Agreement
approved by _____% of the votes".

severally liable with the grantor for all
unpaid assessments by the Association against
the latter for his share of the common expenses
up to the time of the grant or conveyance,
without prejudice to the grantee's right to
recover from the grantor the amounts paid by
the grantee therefor. However, any such
grantee shall be entitled to a statement from
the manager or Board of Directors of the
Association, as the case may be, setting forth
the amount of the unpaid assessments against
the grantor due the Association and such
grantee shall not be liable for, nor shall the
family unit conveyed be subject to a lien
for, any unpaid assessments made by the
Association against the grantor in excess of
the amount therein set forth.

O. All agreements and determinations lawfully
made by the Association in accordance with
the voting percentages established in the ____
_____,* this Declaration or in the
By-Laws, shall be deemed to be binding on all
owners of family units, their successors and
assigns.

P. That the Board of Directors of the Association
of Owners, or the Management Agent, or Manager
shall obtain and continue in effect blanket
property insurance in form and amounts satisfactory to mortgagees holding first mortgages
covering family units but without prejudice
to the right of the owner of a family unit
to obtain individual family unit insurance.

Q. That insurance premiums for any blanket insurance coverage shall be a common expense
to be paid by monthly assessments levied by
the Association of Owners; and that such
payments shall be held in a separate escrow
account of the Association of Owners and
used solely for the payment of the blanket

---

*Identifying state law establishing family unit ownership
if any.

property insurance premiums as such premiums
become due.

R. That so long as said Grantor, its successors
and assigns, owns one or more of the family
units established and described herein, said
Grantor, its successors and assigns shall be
subject to the provisions of this Declaration
and of Exhibits "A", "B", and "C" attached
hereto; and said Grantor covenants to take
no action which would adversely affect the
rights of the Association with respect to
assurances against latent defects in the
property or other right assigned to the
Association, the members of such association
and their successors in interest, as their
interests may appear, by reason of the establishment of the condominium.

S. The terms "Declaration" and "Condominium
Ownership" as used herein shall mean and
include the terms "Master Deed" and "Apartment Ownership" respectively.

(Execution and Acknowledgement
in Accordance with Requirements
of Jurisdiction)

VI. Contract Of Sale

VI. Contract Of Sale

The Subscription and Purchase Agreement is both a contract of sale and a prospectus. It should contain all the information the buyer, his attorney and his potential mortgagor will ever want to ask about a particular development.

A model copy will be found at the end of the chapter.

The prime concern of the buyer is his money. The Agreement spells out first, the exact price of the unit and the amount of down payment which will be required.

It should specifically state that such down payments will be held in escrow or in a trust account until the seller fulfills certain obligations. When these obligations are completed (usually after a certain date or after a specified

CONTRACT OF SALE

number of units has been sold) the seller may, in some cases, have access to the money for construction costs. In most instances, however, the down payment is reserved until the unit is delivered. If the developer is unable to meet the conditions, the buyer's down payment must be refunded.

Another section of the Agreement details the percentage or share in the expenses of the common facilities which will be assigned to each unit.

It further states that a copy of the Master Deed/Enabling Declaration, the By-Laws, and a list of the proposed maintenance costs for the common areas must have been made available to the buyer before he makes the down payment.

The purchase contract sometimes includes a list of lending agencies that are willing to finance mortgages on the units, but it is the duty of the buyer to make his own credit arrangements. The purchaser does not have to use the banks or lending agencies listed.

Under some conditions (strikes, fire, unavailability of key materials) the seller may not be able to deliver the unit by the specified date. In this case the seller's requirements on delivery may be extended by the amount of time lost to such delays, for which he was not responsible.

Also, in the event that the conveyance of title
is delayed because one or more of the initial
provisions cannot be met by the seller, the time
for corrections to be made may be extended 60 days
if both buyer and seller consent to this in
writing. Otherwise, the buyer is eligible for a
full refund.

The responsibility of the seller for fire and
liability insurance on the buildings and common
elements, before and after delivery of individual
units, is included. It is also provided that
coverage on these becomes a part of the general
maintenance charges after the units are sold.
(As provided in the Declaration, the owner may
also take out his own insurance policy written
to apply solely to his unit.)

When the buyer accepts his unit he must pay a
certain percentage of the yearly maintenance costs,
taxes, etc., depending upon the time he took legal
possession.

In the early stages of condominium construction,
before the laws were adequately codified and en-
forced, many of these restrictions were not included
in the purchaser's agreement. This may still be
partially true with developments which are not
built to comply with the FHA Apartment Owner's
Act--in other words, condominiums which will not be
eligible for federal mortgage insurance.

CONTRACT OF SALE

State agencies, however, also have their own regulations on such projects, and if the buyers are not aware of what to check in the agreement of sale, the lenders are, so most contracts cover the areas discussed in this chapter and in the model agreement which follows.

Therefore, the developer who wants his units to attract buyers and mortgage money will make sure his prospectus for sale and purchase agreement adequately cover the requirements.

CONTRACT OF SALE

MODEL FORM OF SUBSCRIPTION AND PURCHASE AGREEMENT*

(Section 234, National Housing Act)

(To be executed in triplicate, one copy with indicated attachments to be retained by the Subscriber.)

Application No. _____

Family Unit No. _____

Project _____

Date _____

WHEREAS, _____ (hereinafter called Seller) is the owner of (or proposes to construct) a multifamily housing project known as _____ located at _____ and WHEREAS, the said project is proposed to be converted to a Condominium; And

WHEREAS, 80 percent of the total value of the family units in the project (or such lesser percent as may be approved by the Federal Housing Administration (hereinafter referred to as the FHA) must be sold to purchasers approved by the FHA before its insurance of individual mortgages under Section 234(c) of the National Housing Act; and

WHEREAS, it will be necessary to establish an association of owners for the operation and regulation of the "common areas and facilities" of the Condominium;

---

*This form is required in cases where subscriber seeks an insured mortgage under Section 234.

CONTRACT OF SALE

BE IT AGREED AS FOLLOWS:

1. Subscription and Purchase Amount

I/We _____, in consideration
of the mutual promises of other subscribers and
other good and valuable considerations, and having
a bona fide intention to reside in a unit in the
above-referred-to project, hereby subscribe for
participation in _____ (herein-
after called Association) and hereby agree to
purchase the above-numbered family unit and the
_____ percentage undivided interest in the
common areas and facilities* for the price of
$_____, payable as follows: $ _____
within _____ days after date hereof and the
balance at time of conveyance as provided in
paragraph 3, hereof.
Seller hereby agrees that all sums received on
account of the purchase of the family unit shall
be held in trust and shall be placed in escrow
account with _____
Bank under an escrow agreement, the terms of which
are acceptable to the FHA. The escrow agreement
shall provide that Seller shall not be entitled to
receive any sums in the escrow until conveyance of
title. I/We hereby subscribe to the Plan of
Apartment Ownership, Association By-Laws and
Regulatory Agreement, copies of which are attached
hereto and receipt of which is hereby acknowledged.
I/We hereby agree that, in addition to the purchase
price above mentioned, I/We will be liable for our
proportionate share of the Association assessments
as outlined in the By-Laws. I/We also agree that
in addition to the above-mentioned purchase price
we will pay to the Association at or before conveyance of title the sum of $_____,
representing our proportionate share of the
Association's required working capital.

2. Plan and Purpose

_____

*References hereinafter made to "family unit" shall in-
clude the undivided interest in the common areas and facilities

The Association will be established for the purpose
of operating and maintaining the common areas and
facilities of the Condominium. Each owner of a
family unit in the Condominium will be a member of
the Association and will be subject to the By-Laws
and regulations thereof. As set forth in the
Plan of Apartment Ownership, the vote of each
member will be based on the ratio of the value of
the family unit(s) which he owns to the total value
of the entire project.
The affairs of the Association will be conducted
by a Board of Directors as provided for in the By-
Laws.

3. Conveyance of Title

In consideration of this subscription the Seller
agrees to convey to Subscriber good and marketable
title to said family unit. Subscriber agrees to
purchase said family unit from the Seller within
thirty (30) days after Seller has notified Subscriber it is prepared to tender title and possession thereof to him for an amount equal to the
purchase price. It is contemplated that the unpaid purchase price will be secured by an individual
mortgage on the family unit by the FHA under Section
234. Subscriber may, however, pay this amount in
cash or may elect to finance under a conventional
uninsured mortgage. It is understood that Subscriber
will, at the time title is conveyed to him, pay such
closing costs as are customarily paid by the purchaser of comparable real estate in this jurisdiction and taxes, assessments and insurance will be
adjusted to the date of closing. The FHA estimate
of value of the above-described family unit is
$_____.

4. Location of Project

The above-referred-to housing project will be
located at _____ in the
City of _____. Nearest public
transportation in the form of (bus, streetcar,
subway, train service)* is available at the
_____

*Strike out inappropriate reference.

CONTRACT OF SALE

following points: _____
Churches, schools, shopping centers, playgrounds and
other community facilities available to members of
the project are located as follows:

_____
_____
_____

5. Priority of Mortgage Lien

This Agreement and all rights hereunder are and at
all times shall be subject and subordinate to the
lien of the mortgage and accompanying documents to
be executed by the Subscriber to a lending insti-
tution and to be insured under Section 234 of the
National Housing Act, and to any and all modifications, extensions, and renewals thereof, and to any
mortgage or deed of trust made in place thereof.

6. Cancellation Rights

In the event Subscriber shall have died prior to
his acquisition of title to the family unit, the
Seller reserves the right to return such amount or
amounts to Subscriber's estate or legal representative, and thereupon all rights of Subscriber shall
cease and terminate without further liability on the
part of the Seller.
It is understood that Subscriber's credit is subject
to approval by the Federal Housing Administration.
In the event the FHA determines that Subscriber
does not meet its credit requirements for participation in this project or Subscriber is unable to
obtain an FHA-insured mortgage thereupon within
        days from date hereof, seller shall
have privilege of withdrawal from this contract and
the Seller shall return to Subscriber all of the
sums paid hereunder and this Agreement shall be
deemed null and void and all of the Subscriber's
and Seller's right shall cease and terminate without further liability on the part of either party.
If Subscriber within five (5) days after the
execution of this Agreement notifies the Seller in
writing that Subscriber wishes to withdraw from
this agreement, the amounts theretofore paid by him

under this Agreement will be returned to him and thereupon all rights and liabilities of Subscriber hereunder shall cease and terminate. The right of the Subscriber to withdraw shall, however, expire unless exercised within such five (5) days period, except that if title to the family unit is not conveyed to the Subscriber in accordance with FHA requirements on or before   , the Subscriber and the Seller shall have the right to withdraw from this agreement, in which event Seller shall return to Subscriber all sums paid hereunder and Subscriber's and Seller's rights shall cease and terminate without further liability on the part of either party.

If the Subscriber shall default in any of the payments or obligations called for in this Agreement, and such default shall continue for fifteen (15) days after notice sent by registered mail by the Seller to the Subscriber at the address given below, then, forthwith at the option of the Seller, the Subscriber shall lose any and all rights under this Agreement, and any amount paid toward the purchase price may be retained by the Seller as liquidated damages, or may at the option of the Seller be returned less the Subscriber's proportionate share of expenses to be determined solely by the Seller. The Seller, may, at its option, release the obligations of Subscriber under this Agreement in the event Subscriber shall secure another subscriber who is satisfactory to the Seller and to the Federal Housing Administration. This agreement is not otherwise assignable.

7. Function of FHA in Connection with this Project

The FHA as insurer of the individual mortgage loan covering a family unit does not insure Subscriber against loss. The validity of title is the responsibility of the Seller and the parties to the mortgage transaction and not of the FHA. FHA has not examined or approved any advertising or informational material in connection with this project other than that contained in this Subscription of Purchase Agreement.

8. Oral Representations Not to be Relied Upon

This Agreement will supersede any and all under-
standings and agreements and constitutes the entire
agreement between the parties and no oral represen-
tations or statements shall be considered a part
hereof.

9. Types of Dwelling Units Available

Attached hereto as Exhibit "A" is a listing of the
various family units in connection with this project,
showing types, cash down payment requirements,
estimated monthly assessments by the Association
and estimated monthly mortgage payments, inclusive
of deposits for mortgage insurance premiums and
taxes, which will be applicable in the event individual
mortgages are insured under Section 234 of the National
Housing Act.

10. Interim Occupancy on Rental Basis

You as a subscriber may, if you desire, move into
the completed dwelling unit prior to conversion of
the project to condominium ownership, provided the
proposed Seller permits you to do so and the FHA
approves such interim occupancy. If you do so,
however, you should be mindful of the fact that prior
to passage of title you will be occupying the premises
merely as a tenant of the proposed Seller and you are
therefore advised not to expend any sums for improvements without a written agreement and authority from
the proposed Seller satisfactory to you as to the
manner in which compensation or adjustments will be
made for such expenditures in the event the conversion to condominium ownership does not ultimately
materialize.

_____
(Subscriber)

WITNESS:

_____

98

CONTRACT OF SALE

_____
(Subscriber)

_____
(Address)

_____
(Telephone)

_____
(Name of Corporation)

_____
(Address)

_____
(Telephone)

_____
(President or other Corporation
officer)

_____
(Address)

_____
(Telephone)

VII. By-Laws

VII. By-Laws

The By-Laws take up where the Declaration leaves off. The Enabling Declaration/Master Deed covers the details of building and developing a comdominium. The By-Laws deal with the responsibilities of the owner-elected Board of Directors.

This Board, chosen from among all members of the Association of Apartment Owners, gradually assumes operation of the project from the developers, beginning at the time a stated percentage of units is sold. When all stages of development are completed, the Board of Directors becomes the executive body in charge of the property.

The By-Laws are also binding upon the owners. The Board oversees enforcement of the rules and regulations accepted by the owners when they signed the purchase agreement.

BY-LAWS

In most cases the developers serve as trustees
with power to make decisions before there is
owner representation. It is considered ideal if
the Board controls the decision-making process
after 51 percent of the units are sold. The By-
Laws usually contain a specific statement regarding
the date of the first owners' meeting.

Day-to-day operation procedures are also a
part of the By-Laws, including methods of collection for the common property assessments, guidelines for repair work and replacement, and information on the Board's duties with regard to hiring
the personnel necessary for smooth operation.

The By-Laws may be amended as particular
needs arise. Amendment rules are not as strict
as with the Master Deed. Usually a simple majority
is needed, but the different state regulations may
vary. Some require up to 66 percent to pass an
amendment. Others don't have a minimum requirement

The first sections of the By-Laws state the
location of the office of the Association of
Apartment Owners, what dates constitute the fiscal
year, and the date of the annual members' meeting,
with provisions for special meetings on demand.

Voting rights of members, proxies, and the
order of business for annual meetings are covered.
Each member must be advised in writing of the date

and place of any meeting a stated number of days
before it will occur. If condominium business
is to be conducted for the best interests of all
the owners, each one should consider it his duty
to attend any and all such meetings.

Regulations on the election of the Board of
Directors (in some state codes called the Board
of Governors or the Trustees) and stipulations
as to their duties, are sections of importance
to both developers and owners. They include the
procedures on assessments, maintenance, insurance,
reconstruction of damaged areas, and the payment
of taxes, utilities, casualty and fire insurance
premiums on the common areas and the employees.

The By-Laws also list the records which should
be kept. These include a roll of apartment owners
and their percentages of assessments, a budget,
copies of the annual audit, and designation of
the bank where all monies are deposited.

A separate list of rules and regulations,
which may be amended more easily than either the
By-Laws or the Master Deed, is usually an addendum
to the By-Laws. It sets general guidelines on
what is expected of the owners in regard to
establishing a favorable image in the community.

These regulations concern minor issues which,
if not spelled out, can become troublesome bones

of contention. They cover the courtesy issues
such as proper parking, keeping children in the
play areas, obstruction of sidewalks or public
areas, excessive decoration, loud music, and, in
some cases, forbid leasing of an apartment without the consent of the Board.

This "add-on" to the By-Laws may seem like a
minor thing, but, as the old saying goes, it's
the little things that count. A seemingly small
annoyance may be the breeding ground for larger
disagreements which might be avoided if the ground
rules are known.

Another possible outcome of the separate
regulations is that they tend to preserve and
foster the conduct which leads to an individual
atmosphere for each development. They can be the
basis for an *esprit de corps* ; a feeling of "this is
our community, these are our rules, and this is
just the way we want it".

Developers who can create this sort of
community atmosphere won't have any trouble filling
other projects. The word will get around.

BY-LAWS

ARTICLE I

PLAN OF APARTMENT OWNERSHIP

Section 1. <u>Apartment Ownership</u>. The project
located at _____ Street, City of __
_____, State of _____, known
as "_____ Condominium" is
submitted to the provisions of*_____

Section 2. <u>By-Laws Applicability</u>. The provisions
of these By-Laws are applicable to the project.
(The term "project" as used herein shall include
the land.)

Section 3. <u>Personal Application</u>. All present or
future owners, tenants, future tenants, or their
employees, or any other person that might use the
facilities of the project in any manner, are
subject to the regulations set forth in these By-
Laws and to the Regulatory Agreement, attached as
Exhibit "C" to the recorded Plan of Apartment
Ownership.

The mere acquisition or rental of any of the family
units (hereinafter referred to as "units") of the
project or the mere act of occupancy of any of
said units will signify that these By-Laws and
the provisions of the Regulatory Agreement are
accepted, ratified, and will be complied with.

ARTICLE II

VOTING, MAJORITY OF OWNERS, QUORUM, PROXIES

Section 1. <u>Voting</u>. Voting shall be on a percent-

_____

*Identify state law establishing apartment ownership.

age basis and the percentage of the vote to which the owner is entitled is the percentage assigned to the family unit or units in the Master Deed.

Section 2. Majority of Owners. As used in these By-Laws the term "majority of owners" shall mean those owners holding 51% of the votes in accordance with the percentages assigned in the Master Deed.

Section 3. Quorum. Except as otherwise provided in these By-Laws, the presence in person or by proxy of a "majority of owners" as defined in Section 2 of this Article shall constitute a quorum.

Section 4. Proxies. Votes may be cast in person or by proxy. Proxies must be filed with the Secretary before the appointed time of each meeting.

ARTICLE III

ADMINISTRATION

Section 1. Association Responsibilities. The owners of the units will constitute the Association of Owners (hereinafter referred to as "Association") who will have the responsibility of administering the project, approving the annual budget, establishing and o llecting monthly assessments and arranging for the management of the project pursuant to an agreement, containing provisions relating to the duties, obligations, removal and compensation of the management agent. Except as otherwise provided, decisions and resolutions of the Association shall require approval by a majority of owners.

Section 2. Place of Meetings. Meetings of the Association shall be held at the principal office of the project or such other suitable place convenient to the owners as may be designated by the Board of Directors.

Section 3. Annual Meetings. The first annual
meeting of the Association shall be held on _____
_____ (Date)*. Thereafter, the annual meetings
of the Association shall be held on the _____
(1st, 2nd, 3rd, 4th) _____ (Monday,
Tuesday, Wednesday, etc.) of _____
(month) each succeeding year. At such meetings
there shall be elected by ballot of the owners a
Board of Directors in accordance with the requirements of Section 5 of Article IV of these By-Laws.
The owners may also transact such other business
of the Association as may properly come before them

Section 4. Special Meetings. It shall be the duty
of the President to call a special meeting of the
owners as directed by resolution of the Board of
Governors or upon a petition signed by a majority
of the owners and having been presented to the
Secretary, or at the request of the Federal Housing
Commissioner or his duly authorized representative.
The notice of any special meeting shall state the
time and place of such meeting and the purpose
thereof. No business shall be transacted at a
special meeting except as stated in the notice
unless by consent of four-fifths of the owners
present, either in person or by proxy.

Section 5. Notice of Meetings. It shall be the
duty of the Secretary to mail a notice of each
annual or special meeting, stating the purpose
thereof as well as the time and place where it is
to be held, to each owner of record, at least 5
but not more than 10 days prior to such meeting.
The mailing of a notice in the manner provided in
this Section shall be considered notice served.
Notices of all meetings shall be mailed to the
Director of the local insuring office of the
Federal Housing Administration.

Section 6. Adjourned Meetings. If any meeting
of owners cannot be organized because a quorum has
not attended, the owners who are present, either

_____

*This date must be approved by the FHA Insuring Office.

109

in person or by proxy, may adjourn the meeting to
a time not less than forty-eight (48) hours from
the time the original meeting was called.

Section 7. Order of Business. The order of
business at all meetings of the owners of units
shall be as follows:

    (a) Roll call.
    (b) Proof of notice of meeting or waiver
        of notice.
    (c) Reading of minutes of preceding meeting.
    (d) Reports of officers.
    (e) Report of Federal Housing Administration
        representative, if present.
    (f) Report of committees.
    (g) Election of inspectors of election.
    (h) Election of directors.
    (i) Unfinished business.
    (j) New business.

ARTICLE IV

BOARD OF DIRECTORS

Section 1. Number and Qualification. The affairs
of the Association shall be governed by a Board
of Directors composed of _____ persons,*
all of whom must be owners of units in the project

Section 2. Powers and Duties. The Board of
Directors shall have the powers and duties necessary for the administration of the affairs of the
Association and may do all such acts and things
as are not by law or by these By-Laws directed to
be exercised and done by the owners.

Section 3. Other Duties. In addition to duties
imposed by these By-Laws or by resolutions of the
Association, the Board of Directors shall be

---

*The number should be an odd number not less than five

responsible for the following:

(a) Care, upkeep and surveillance of the
project and the common areas and
facilities and the restricted common
areas and facilities.

(b) Collection of monthly assessments from
the owners.

(c) Designation and dismissal of the personnel necessary for the maintenance
and operation of the project, the
common areas and facilities and the
restricted common areas and facilities.

Section 4. Management Agent. The Board of
Directors may employ for the Association a manage-
ment agent at a compensation established by the
Board to perform such duties and services as the
Board shall authorize including, but not limited
to, the duties listed in Section 3 of this
Article.

Section 5. Election and Term of Office. At the
first annual meeting of the Association the term
of office of two Directors shall be fixed for
three (3) years. The term of office of two
Directors shall be fixed at two (2) years, and
the term of office of one Director shall be fixed
at one (1) year. At the expiration of the initial
term of office of each respective Director, his
successor shall be elected to serve a term of
three (3) years. The Directors shall hold office
until their successors have been elected and hold
their first meeting. (If a larger Board of
Directors is contemplated, the terms of office
should be established in a similar manner so that
they will expire in different years.)

Section 6. Vacancies. Vacancies in the Board
of Directors caused by any reason other than the
removal of a Director by a vote of the Association shall be filled by vote of the majority of
the remaining Directors, even though they may
constitute less than a quorum; and each person so
elected shall be a Director until a successor is
elected at the next annual meeting of the

Association.

Section 7. Removal of Directors. At any regular or special meeting duly called, any one or more of the Directors may be removed with or without cause by a majority of the owners and a successor may then and there be elected to fill the vacancy thus created. Any Director whose removal has been proposed by the owners shall be given an opportunity to be heard at the meeting.

Section 8. Organization Meeting. The first meeting of a newly elected Board of Directors shall be held within ten (10) days of election at such place as shall be fixed by the Directors at the meeting at which such Directors were elected, and no notice shall be necessary to the newly elected Directors in order legally to constitute such meeting, providing a majority of the whole Board shall be present.

Section 9. Regular Meetings. Regular meetings of the Board of Directors may be held at such time and place as shall be determined, from time to time, by a majority of the Directors, but at least two such meetings shall be held during each fiscal year. Notice of regular meetings of the Board of Directors shall be given to each Director, personally or by mail, telephone or telegraph, at least three (3) days prior to the day named for such meeting.

Section 10. Special Meetings. Special meetings of the Board of Directors may be called by the President on three days notice to each Director, given personally or by mail, telephone or telegraph, which notice shall state the time, place (as here-inabove provided) and purpose of the meeting. Special meetings of the Board of Directors shall be called by the President or Secretary in like manner and on like notice on the written request of at least three Directors.

Section 11. Waiver of Notice. Before or at any meeting of the Board of Directors, any Director may, in writing, waive notice of such meeting and such waiver shall be deemed equivalent to the giving of such notice. Attendance by a Director at any meeting of the Board shall be required and any business may be transacted at such meeting.

Section 12. Board of Directors' Quorum. At all meetings of the Board of Directors, a majority of the Directors shall constitute a quorum for the transaction of business, and the acts of the majority of the Directors present at a meeting at which a quorum is present shall be the acts of the Board of Directors. If, at any meeting of the Board of Directors, there be less than a quorum present, the majority of those present may adjourn the meeting from time to time. At any such adjourned meeting, any business which might have been transacted at the meeting as originally called may be transacted without further notice.

Section 13. Fidelity Bonds. The Board of Directors shall require that all officers and employees of the Association handling or responsible for Association funds shall furnish adequate fidelity bonds. The premiums on such bonds shall be paid by the Association.

ARTICLE V

OFFICERS

Section 1. Designation. The principal officers of the Association shall be a President, a Vice President, a Secretary, and a Treasurer, all of whom shall be elected by and from the Board of Directors. The Directors may appoint an assistant treasurer, and an assistant secretary, and such other officers as in their judgment may be necessary. (In the case of an Association of one hundred owners or less the offices of Treasurer and Secretary may be filled by the same person.)

Section 2. Election of Officers. The Officers of

113

the Association shall be elected annually by the
Board of Directors at the organization meeting of
each new Board and shall hold office at the
pleasure of the Board.

Section 3. <u>Removal of Officers</u>. Upon an affirma-
tive vote of a majority of the members of the
Board of Directors, any officer may be removed,
either with or without cause, and his successor
elected at any regular meeting of the Board of
Directors, or at any special meeting of the
Board called for such purpose.

Section 4. <u>President</u>. The President shall be the
chief executive officer of the Association. He
shall preside at all meetings of the Association
and of the Board of Directors. He shall have all
of the general powers and duties which are usually
vested in the office of president of an Association,
including but not limited to the power to appoint
committees from among the owners from time to
time as he may in his discretion decide is appropriate to assist in the conduct of the affairs of
the Association.

Section 5. <u>Vice President</u>. The Vice President
shall take the place of the President and perform
his duties whenever the President shall be absent
or unable to act. If neither the President nor
the Vice President is able to act, the Board of
Directors shall appoint some other member of the
Board to so do on an interim basis. The Vice
President shall also perform such other duties as
shall from time to time be imposed upon him by
the Board of Directors.

Section 6. <u>Secretary</u>. The Secretary shall keep
the minutes of all meetings of the Board of Directors and the minutes of all meetings of the Association; he shall have charge of such books and
papers as the Board of Directors may direct; and
he shall, in general, perform all the duties inci-
dent to the office of Secretary.

Section 7. <u>Treasurer</u>. The Treasurer shall have

responsibility for Association funds and securities and shall be responsible for keeping full and accurate accounts of all receipts and disbursements in books belonging to the Association. He shall be responsible for the deposit of all monies and other valuable effects in the name, and to the credit, of the Association in such depositories as may from time to time be designated by the Board of Directors.

ARTICLE VI

OBLIGATIONS OF THE OWNERS

Section 1. <u>Assessments</u>. All owners are obligated to pay monthly assessments imposed by the Association to meet all project communal expenses, which may include a liability insurance policy premium and an insurance premium for a policy to cover repair and reconstruction work in case of hurricane, fire, earthquake or other hazard. The assessments shall be made pro rata according to the value of the unit owned, as stipulated in the Master Deed. Such assessments shall include monthly payments to a General Operating Reserve and a Reserve Fund for Replacements as required in the Regulatory Agreement attached as Exhibit "C" to the Plan of Apartment Ownership.

Section 2. <u>Maintenance and Repair</u>.

(a) Every owner must perform promptly all maintenance and repair work within his own unit, which if omitted would affect the project in its entirety or in a part belonging to other owners, being expressly responsible for the damages and liabilities that his failure to do so may engender.

(b) All the repairs of internal installations of the unit such as water, light, gas, power, sewage, telephones, air conditioners, sanitary installations, doors, windows, lamps and all other accessories belonging to the unit area shall be at the owner's expense.

Section 3.   Use of Family Units - Internal Changes.

(a) All units shall be utilized for residential purposes only.

(b) An owner shall not make structural modifications or alterations in his unit or installations located therein without previously notifying the Association in writing, through the Management Agent, if any, or through the President of the Board of Directors, if no management agent is employed. The Association shall have the obligation to answer within   days and failure to do so within the stipulated time shall mean that there is no objection to the proposed modification or alteration.

Section 4.   Use of Common Areas and Facilities and Restricted Common Areas and Facilities.

(a) An owner shall not place or cause to be placed in the lobbies, vestibules, stairways, elevators and other project areas and facilities of a similar nature both common and restricted, any furniture, packages or objects of any kind. Such areas shall be used for no other purpose than for normal transit through them.

(b) The project shall have _____ elevators, _____ devoted to the transportation of the owners and their guests and _____ for freight service, or auxiliary purposes. Owners and tradesmen are expressly required to utilize exclusively a freight or service elevator for transporting packages, merchandise or any other object that may affect the comfort or well-being of the passengers of the elevator dedicated to the transportation of owners, residents and guests.

Section 5.   Right of Entry.

116

(a) An owner shall grant the right of entry to the management agent or to any other person authorized by the Board of Directors or the Association in case of any emergency originating in or threatening his unit, whether the owner is present at the time or not.

(b) An owner shall permit other owners, or their representatives, when so required, to enter his unit for the purpose of performing installations, alterations or repairs to the mechanical or electrical services, provided that requests for entry are made in advance and that such entry is at a time convenient to the owner. In case of an emergency, such right of entry shall be immediate.

Section 6. <u>Rules of Conduct.</u>

(a) No resident of the project shall post any advertisements, or posters of any kind in or on the project except as authorized by the Association.

(b) Residents shall exercise extreme care about making noises or the use of musical instruments, radios, television and amplifiers that may disturb other residents. Keeping domestic animals will abide by the Municipal Sanitary Regulations.

(c) It is prohibited to hang garments, rugs, etc., from the windows or from any of the facades of the project.

(d) It is prohibited to dust rugs, etc., from the windows, or to clean rugs, etc., by beating on the exterior part of the project.

(e) It is prohibited to throw garbage or trash outside the disposal installations provided for such purposes in the service areas.

(f) No owner, resident or lessee shall install wiring for electrical or telephone installation, television antennae,

machines or air conditioning units, etc.,
on the exterior of the project or that
protrude through the walls or the roof
of the project except as authorized by
the Association.

ARTICLE VII

AMENDMENTS TO PLAN OF APARTMENT OWNERSHIP

Section 1. By-Laws. These By-Laws may be amended
by the Association in a duly constituted meeting
for such purpose and no amendment shall take effect
unless approved by owners representing at least
75% of the total value of all units in the project
as shown in the Master Deed.

ARTICLE VIII

MORTGAGEES

Section 1. Notice to Association. An owner who
mortgages his unit, shall notify the Association
through the Management Agent, if any, or the
President of the Board of Directors in the event
there is no Management Agent, the name and address
of his mortgagee; and the Association shall maintain such information in a book entitled "Mortgagees
of Units".

Section 2. Notice of Unpaid Assessments. The
Association shall at the request of a mortgagee
of a unit report any unpaid assessments due from
the owner of such unit.

ARTICLE IX

COMPLIANCE

These By-Laws are set forth to comply with the

requirements of*

In case any of these By-Laws conflict with the
provisions of said statute, it is hereby agreed
and accepted that the provisions of the statute
will apply.

---

*Identify state law establishing apartment ownership.

VIII. Management And Budget

VIII. Management And Budget

The question of a sound fiscal policy for a
projected development, both during and after
construction, are of legitimate concern to the
developer and the buyer.

The By-Laws provide for hiring a management
firm to take care of the financial affairs of a
condominium in the development stage. When the
Association of Apartment Owners receives the
property it may either keep the team used by the
developers or make arrangements to employ one of
their own choosing.

The management team's first responsibility
to the developer is to draw up an operating budget
to be included in the purchase and sales agreement
so prospective buyers can get a clear idea of the
breakdown of the monthly charges. After the
changeover they collect the monthly assessments;

maintain the property, and are in charge of
employees needed to service the common facilities.

The FHA requires that a management firm be
selected and lending institutions also prefer to
cover their investment by an assurance that the
condominium's interests are being served by a
professional staff.

Under FHA regulations the management contract
should not run for more than one year at a time,
with provision for a change, if necessary, after
30 days notice by either party. This is particularly
important in case the owners wish to change the
firm hired by the developers after the Board of
Directors is elected.

The agreement should state exactly what areas
of responsibility will be within the duties of
the management agent. One member of the Board is
made a liaison officer to give the manager instructions and bring his questions to the Directors.

All information regarding the time period the
management agreement will be in effect and conditions
of its termination or renewal are included.

Other provisions deal with the preparation of
the annual budget and state the manager's duties
in regard to dispensing funds, including limits

on amounts to be spent on any given item of repair
or alteration without further approval by the
Board. A clause is usually included to give the
manager authority to act in emergencies without
having written consent.

The management firm is expected to prepare
statements for the Board at the end of each month,
listing collections, disbursements, salaries of
the agent and his staff and a report of funds held
in reserve.

A management agent should be able to present
to the Board of Directors at the first annual
meeting, or shortly thereafter, the techniques
of condominium management and explain the interlocking responsibilities of his office, the unit
owners and the Board.

In addition to these duties, he is usually
also accountable for collection of all bills due
the Apartment Association. He must file the
necessary tax and insurance forms, maintain a
complete inventory of condominium property, and
be able, at a moment's notice, to put his hands
on any document that may be requested regarding
the business operations.

All duties of the management agent and his
employees are equivalent to the responsibilities
of what would be called the business office in

other organizations. He sometimes is also empowered to act as the selling agent for the condominium,
depending on how the contract is written.

An FHA Model Management Agreement follows at
the end of this chapter. It is recommended that
only very small condominiums without extensive
common elements try to get by without a management
contract.

BUDGETING

In the case of a new development, only projec-
tions can be made of the budget and it is absolutely
necessary to have this done by a professional management firm, preferably, one with a great deal of
experience in the field. Anyone without such
experience can easily under- or overestimate the
monthly charges, which can lead to lost sales and
disgruntled owners.

Costs are usually grouped under four categories:
operation and maintenance, management costs, fixed
expenses, and reserve funds.

The first, operation and maintenance, includes
utilities (electricity, gas, sewer and water),
janitorial service, trash collection, building
and grounds maintenance and security.

The breakdown of management costs should show
the monies necessary for the expenses of the
management firm, legal counsel and outside account-

ing costs (yearly audits, etc.).

Fixed expenses and Reserve funds complete the list. Under fixed expenses are insurance and other set fees, such as retainers. Any well-managed condominium has reserves set aside for unexpected major repairs, and replacement of furnishings in the common areas. Other funds should be available in the case of future cost increases not foreseeable when the budget was established.

Both lenders and prospective buyers will want to know that the expenses listed are realistic. They are within their rights to ask searching questions about the breakdown of projected costs and how they compare with other developments.

Some will ask how the real estate taxes and mortgage interest were figured, and by whom. If the description of the monthly assessment is not sufficiently detailed, there will be inquiries on that, too.

A careful study of the proposed budget which follows will provide the prospective developer with a place to start.

MORTGAGE INSURANCE

Potential lenders look closely at the reserve

and contingency funds set aside in the budget of
a potential condominium. FHA looks even more
closely, to the extent that in order to qualify
for mortgage insurance approval, the developer
must show that these reserves are large enough to
cover damages and cost of replacement of items
which, if not repaired, would decrease the value
of the condominium as a whole.

Lenders want assurance that their investment
won't be jeopardized by lack of money to cover
expensive structural replacements caused by
mechanical obsolescence (heating plant, roofs,
siding) or by maltreatment of separate units by
careless owners, leading to diminished value on
resale.

In addition to inclusion of these projected
expenses as regular budget items, FHA requires
the developer to list reserve and contingency
funds on a Mortgage Regulator Agreement (repro-
duced at the end of this chapter). The more
conservative building finance institutions, although not bound by FHA standards, will want to
be sure that steps have been taken to maintain
the value of both individual units and the
common areas during the time their mortgages are
in force.

Item 1 of the Regulator Agreement shows just
how much of the reserve fund is set aside for

structural replacement, as distinguished from
maintenance, and what percentage of the unit-
owner assessments are to be set aside for this
purpose. This section covers the responsibility
of developers toward the maintenance of property
values.

The second section deals with unit-owner
responsibilities, or lack of them. It provides
for a contingency fund to cover losses or damage
involving individual units. For example, an
owner or a number of owners with financial problems may fall behind in their mortgage payments.
They will also, at the same time, fall behind in
their condominium assessments. Until the situation
is resolved and they either make up the arrears
or sell the property, the expenses for which these
assessments are made continue, and must be paid.
An adequate contingency fund should be large enough
to provide for such situations.

This reserve is also used to rehabilitate
units which have not been properly maintained by
the owners prior to foreclosure or departure for
any reason. If there is no fund set aside to
repair owner-damaged premises, the value of the
entire project diminishes. Mortgage companies
and banks will not want to rehabilitate property
before resale, and a prospective buyer will demand
a cut in price (thus depressing values in the
condominium as a whole) if he is expected to

repair the former owner's neglect.

Some developers build up this fund by re-
quiring an advance security deposit (returnable)
equal to two or three months common charges.
Others earmark a certain percentage of the owner's
share of the assessments. How it's done is not
as important as making sure such funds will exist.

MODEL FORM OF MANAGEMENT AGREEMENT FOR CONDOMINIUMS

(Section 234)

Agreement made this _____ day of _____, 19____, between the * _____ _____ for the _____ Condominium, hereinafter called the "Association" organized and established in accordance with the Plan of Apartment Ownership executed and recorded in the Office of the Recorder of the County of _____, State of _____, in Book of _____ Deeds at page _____, having its principal office at _____, and _____, havings its principal office at _____, hereinafter called the "Agent".

WITNESSETH:

In consideration of the terms, conditions, and covenants hereinafter set forth, the parties hereto mutually agree as follows:

FIRST. (a) The Association hereby appoints the Agent, and the Agent hereby accepts appointment, on the terms and conditions hereinafter provided, as exclusive managing agent of the condominium known as _____, located in the County of _____, State of _____, and consisting of _____ dwelling units.

(b) The Agent fully understands that the function of the Association is the operation and management of the Condominium; and the Agent agrees, notwithstanding the authority given to the Agent in this Agreement, to confer fully and freely with the Directors of the Association in the performance of its duties as herein set forth and to attend membership or Directors' meetings at any

_____

*Name of association, cooperative or corporation of unit owners.

time or times requested by the Association. It
is further understood and agreed that the authority
and duties conferred upon the Agent hereunder are
confined to the common areas and facilities and
the restricted common areas and facilities as
defined in the Plan of Apartment Ownership. Such
authority and duties do not and shall not include
supervision or management of family units except
as directed by the Association.

SECOND. In order to facilitate efficient
operation, the Association shall furnish the
Agent with a complete set of the plans and specifications of the Condominium as finally approved by
the Federal Housing Administration, and with the
aid of these documents and inspection made by
competent personnel, the Agent will inform itself
with respect to the layout, construction, location,
character, plan and operation of the lighting,
heating, plumbing, and ventilating systems, as
well as elevators, if any, and other mechanical
equipment in the Condominium. Copies of guarantees
and warranties pertinent to the construction of the
Condominium and in force at the time of the execution of this Agreement shall be furnished to the
Agent.

THIRD. The Agent shall hire in its own name
all managerial personnel necessary for the efficient
discharge of the duties of the Agent hereunder.
Compensation for the services of such employees
shall be the responsibility of the Agent. Those
employees of the Agent who handle or are responsible for the handling of the Association's monies
shall, without expense to the Association, be
bonded by a fidelity bond acceptable both to the
Agent and the Association.

FOURTH. Under the personal and direct
supervision of one of its principal officers,
the Agent shall render services and perform duties
as follows:

(a) On the basis of an operating schedule,
job standards and wage rates previously approved

by the Association on the recommendation of the Agent, investigate, hire, pay, supervise, and discharge the personnel necessary to be employed in order properly to maintain and operate the Condominium. Such personnel shall in every instance be in the Association's and not in the Agent's employ. Compensation for the services of such employees (as expressed by certified payrolls) shall be considered an operating expense of the Condominium.

(b) Immediately ascertain the general condition of the property, and if the accommodations there afforded have yet to be occupied for the first time, establish liaison with the general contractor to facilitate the completion by him of such corrective work, if any, as is yet to be done; also, cause an inventory to be taken of all furniture, office equipment, maintenance tools and supplies, including a determination as to the amount of fuel on hand.

(c) Coordinate the plans of owners of family units in the Condominiums, hereinafter referred to as "Members" for moving their personal effects into the Condominium or out of it, with a view towards scheduling such movements so that there shall be a minimum of inconvenience to other Members.

(d) Maintain businesslike relations with Members whose service requests shall be received, considered and recorded in systematic fashion in order to show the action taken with respect to each. Complaints of a serious nature shall, after thorough investigation, be reported to the Association with appropriate recommendations. As part of a continuing program, secure full performance by the Members of all items and maintenance for which they are responsible.

(e) Collect all monthly assessments due from Members, all rents due from users of garage spaces and from users or lessees of other dwelling facilities in the Condominium; also, all sums due from concessionaires in consequence of the authorized operation of facilities in the Condominium maintained primarily for the benefit of the Members. The Association hereby authorizes

the Agent to request, demand, collect, receive,
and receipt for any and all charges or rents
which may at any time be or become due to the
Association and to take such action in the name
of the Association by way of legal process or
otherwise as may be required for the collection
of delinquent monthly assessments. As a standard
practice, the Agent shall furnish the Association
with an itemized list of all delinquent accounts
immediately following the tenth day of each month.

(f) Cause the buildings, appurtenances and
grounds of the Condominium to be maintained
according to standards acceptable to the Association, including but not limited to interior
and exterior cleaning, painting, and decorating,
plumbing, steamfitting, carpentry, and such other
normal maintenance and repair work as may be
necessary, subject to any limitations imposed by
the Association in addition to those contained
herein. For any one item of repair or replacement the expense incurred shall not exceed the
sum of _____* unless specifically
authorized by the Association; excepting, however,
that emergency repairs, involving manifest danger
to life or property, or immediately necessary for
the preservation and safety of the property, or
for the safety of the Members, or required to
avoid the suspension of any necessary service to
the Condominium, may be made by the Agent irrespective of the cost limitation imposed by this
paragraph. Notwithstanding this authority as to
emergency repairs, it is understood and agreed that
the Agent will, if at all possible, confer immediately with the Association regarding every such
expenditure. The Agent shall not incur liabilities
(direct or contingent) which will at any time
exceed the aggregate of _____**, or any
liability maturing more than one year from the
creation thereof, without first obtaining the
approval of the Association.

---

*From $100 to $500, depending upon the size of the
Condominium.

**From $1,000 to $5,000, depending upon the size of
the Condominium.

(g) Take such action as may be necessary to
comply promptly with any and all orders or
requirements affecting the premises placed thereon by any federal, state, county, or municipal
authority having jurisdiction thereover, and orders
of the Board of Fire Underwriters or other similar
bodies, subject to the same limitations contained
in Paragraph (f) of this Article in connection
with the making of repairs and alterations. The
Agent, however, shall not take any action under
this Paragraph (g) so long as the Association is
contesting, or has affirmed its intention to
contest any such order or requirement. The Agent
shall promptly, and in no event later than 72
hours from the time of their receipt, notify the
Association in writing of all such orders and
notices of requirements.

(h) Subject to approval by the Association,
make contracts for water, electricity, gas, fuel
oil, telephone, vermin extermination and other
necessary services, or such of them as the Association shall deem advisable. Also, place orders
for such equipment, tools, appliances, materials
and supplies as are necessary properly to maintain the Condominium. All such contracts and
orders shall be made in the name of the Association
and shall be subject to the limitations set forth
in Paragraph (f) of this Article. When taking
bids or issuing purchase orders, the Agent shall
act at all times under the direction of the
Association, and shall be under a duty to secure
for and credit to the latter any discounts,
commissions, or rebates obtainable as a result of
such purchases.

(i) When authorized by the Association in
writing, cause to be placed and kept in force all
forms of insurance needed adequately to protect
the Association, its members, and mortgagees
holding mortgages covering family units, as their
respective interests appear (or as required by
law), including but not limited to workmen's
compensation insurance, public liability insurance,
boiler insurance, fire and extended coverage
insurance, and burglary and theft insurance. All
of the various types of insurance coverage therein

as shall be acceptable to the Association and to mortgagees holding mortgages covering family units. The Agent shall promptly investigate and make a full written report as to all accidents or claims for damage relating to the management, operation and maintenance of the Condominium, including any damage or destruction to the Condominium, the estimated cost of repair, and shall cooperate and make any and all reports required by any insurance company in connection therewith.

(j) From the funds collected and deposited in the special account hereinafter provided, cause to be disbursed regularly and punctually (1) salaries and any other compensation due and payable to the employees of the Association, and the taxes payable under Paragraph (k) of this Article, (2) fire and other property insurance premiums and the amount specified in the Regulatory Agreement for allocation to the Reserve Fund for Replacements and to the General Operating Reserve, and (3) sums otherwise due and payable by the Association as operating expenses authorized to be incurred under the terms of this Agreement, including the Agent's commission. After disbursement in the order herein specified, any balance remaining in the special account may be disbursed or transferred from time to time, but only as specifically directed by the Association in writing, but such balance must be within the limits of the fidelity bond which shall be in an amount equal to the gross monthly collections.

(k) Working in conjunction with an accountant, prepare for execution and filing by the Association all forms, reports, and returns required by law in connection with unemployment insurance, workmen's compensation insurance, disability benefits, Social Security, and other similar taxes now in effect or hereafter imposed, and also requirements relating to the employment of personnel.

(l) Maintain a comprehensive system of office records, books, and accounts in a manner satisfactory to the Association and to the consenting parties, which records shall be subject to examination by their authorized agents at all reasonable hours. As a standard practice, the Agent shall

render to the Association by not later than the
tenth of each succeeding month a statement of
receipts and disbursements as of the end of
every month.

(m) On or about _____ and thereafter
at least 60 days before the beginning of each
new fiscal year, prepare with the assistance of
an accountant, if need be, an operating budget
setting forth an itemized statement of the anticipated receipts and disbursements for the new fiscal
year based upon the then current schedule of
monthly assessments, and taking into account the
general conditions of the Condominium. Each such
budget, together with a statement from the Agent
outlining a plan of operation and justifying the
estimates made in every important particular,
shall be submitted to the Association in final
draft at least 30 days prior to the commencement
of the annual period for which it has been made,
and following its adoption by the Association,
copies of it shall be made available, upon request,
for submission to the consenting party. The
budget shall serve as a supporting document for
the schedule of monthly assessments proposed for
the new fiscal year. It shall also constitute a
major control under which the Agent shall operate,
and there shall be no substantial variances there-
from, except such as may be sanctioned by the
Association. By this is meant that no expense may
be incurred or commitments made by the Agent in
connection with the maintenance and operation of
the Condominium in excess of the amounts allocated
to the various classifications of expense in the
approved budget without the prior consent of the
Association, except that, if necessary because of
an emergency or lack of sufficient time to obtain
such prior consent, an overrun may be experienced,
provided it is brought promptly to the attention
of the Association in writing.

(n) The Agent shall actively handle the rent-
ing of any garage spaces or other non-dwelling
accommodation, arranging for the execution of
such leases or permits as may be required.*

---

*If desired, a clause may be included whereby the Agent,
upon the request of the owner of any family unit, agrees to
serve as broker or agent in the sales or rentals of individual
family units for a specified commission.

(o) It shall be the duty of the Agent at all times during the term of this Agreement to operate and maintain the Condominium according to the highest standards achievable consistent with the overall plan of the Association and the interests of the consenting party. The Agent shall see that all Members are informed with respect to such rules, regulations and notices as may be promulgated by the Association from time to time. The Agent shall be expected to perform such other acts and deeds as are reasonable, necessary and proper in the discharge of his duties under this Agreement.

FIFTH. Everything done by the Agent under the provisions of Article FOURTH shall be done as Agent of the Association, and all obligations or expenses incurred thereunder shall be for the account, on behalf, and at the expense of the Association, except that the Association shall not be obligated to pay the overhead expenses of the Agent's office. Any payments to be made by the Agent hereunder shall be made out of such sums as are available in the special account of the Association, or as may be provided by the Association. The Agent shall not be obliged to make any advance to or for the account of the Association or to pay any sum, except out of funds held or provided as aforesaid, nor shall the Agent be obliged to incur any liability or obligation for the account of the Association without assurance that the necessary funds for the discharge thereof will be provided.

SIXTH. The Agent shall establish and maintain, in a bank whose deposits are insured by the Federal Deposit Insurance Corporation and in a manner to indicate the custodial nature thereof, a separate bank account as Agent of the Association for the deposit of the monies of the Association, with authority to draw thereon for any payments to be made by the Agent to discharge any liabilities or obligations incurred pursuant to this Agreement, and for the payment of the Agent's fee, all of which payments shall be subject to the limitations in this Agreement.

SEVENTH. The sole compensation which the
Agent shall be entitled to receive for all services
performed under this Agreement shall be a fee
computed and payable monthly in an amount equivalent to _____ (%) of gross collections,
exclusive of all surcharges.

EIGHTH. (a) Unless cancelled pursuant to
action (b), (c), or (d) of this Article, this
Agreement shall be in effect for a term of _____
_____ from the date of execution, provided that
in no event shall it be of any force and effect
until there is endorsed hereon the consent of the
consenting party.
   (b) This Agreement may be terminated by
mutual consent of the parties as of the end of
any calendar month, but not without prior written
notice to the consenting party.
   (c) In the event a petition in bankruptcy is
filed by or against Agent, or in the event that he
shall make an assignment for the benefit of
creditors or take advantage of any insolvency act,
either party hereto may terminate this Agreement
without notice to the other, but prompt advice of
such action shall be given to the consenting party.
   (d) It is expressly understood and agreed by
and between the parties hereto that the Federal
Housing Administration shall have the right to
terminate this Agreement at the end of any calendar
month, with or without cause, on 30 days' written
notice to the Association and the Agent of its
intention so to do. It is further understood and
agreed that no liability shall attach to the
Federal Housing Administration in the event of
termination of this Agreement pursuant to this
section.
   (e) Upon termination, the contracting parties
shall account to each other with respect to all
matters outstanding as of the date of termination,
and the Association shall furnish the Agent security,
satisfactory to the Agent, against any outstanding
obligations or liabilities which the Agent may
have incurred hereunder.

NINTH. As used in this Agreement:

(a) The term "consenting party" shall mean the Federal Housing Administration acting through its Commissioner or his duly authorized representatives.

(b) The term "assessments" shall mean those monthly rates established by the Association which the Members are bound to pay as their share of the common expenses under the Master Plan of Apartment Ownership.

(c) The term "gross collections" shall mean all amounts actually collected by the Agent, either as assessments or as rents.

(d) The term "Association" as used herein shall mean an association, cooperative or corporation consisting of all of the owners of family units in the Condominium organized and existing under state law for the purpose of administering the Condominium established by the Plan of Apartment Ownership.

TENTH. (a) This Agreement, which is made subject and subordinate to all rights of the Federal Housing Administration as insurer of mortgages on family units in the Condominium, shall insure to the benefit of and constitute a binding obligation upon the contracting parties, their respective successors and assigns; and to the extent that it confers rights, privileges, and benefits upon the consenting party, the same shall be deemed to insure to its benefit, but without liability, in the same manner and with the same force and effect as though the Federal Housing Administration was a signatory to this Agreement.

(b) This Agreement shall constitute the entire Agreement between the contracting parties, and no variance or modification thereof shall be valid and enforceable, except by supplemental agreement in writing, executed and approved in the same manner as this Agreement.

(c) For the convenience of the parties, this Agreement has been executed in several counterparts, which are in all respects similar and each

of which shall be deemed to be complete in itself
so that any one may be introduced in evidence or
used for any other purpose without the production
of the other counterparts. Immediately following
endorsement of the consenting parties, counterparts
will be furnished to the consenting parties so
that each may be advised of the rights, privileges,
and benefits which this Agreement confers.

IN WITNESS WHEREOF, the parties hereto have
executed this Agreement the day and year first
above written.

_____
(Association)

By_____

_____
(Agent)

By _____

The Federal Housing Administration hereby consents
to the foregoing Management Agreement and the
Managing Agent designated therein.

Date:_____   _____
                   (Federal Housing Commissioner)

          By _____
                   (Authorized Agent)

141

MANAGEMENT AND BUDGET

ANNUAL OPERATING BUDGET FOR COOPERATIVE HOUSING CORPORATIONS

PROJECT NO. (S) _____

PROJECT NAME _____ ADDRESS _____

COVERING PERIOD FROM _____ TO _____

Expenses	Acct#	1 Prior Year Budget	2 Prior Year Actual	3 Over (Under)	4 Adjust-ments Incr. (Decr.)	5 New Annual Budget	6 Adjust-ments By HUD
1.Vacancy & Col- lection Loss	6370						
2.Employee Apart- ment Rent	6330						
3.Apart- ment Resale Exp.	6200						
4.Manage- ment Fee	6320						
5.Legal Exp.	6340						
6.Audit Exp.	6350						
7.Tele- phone	6360						
8.Office & Adm. Sala- ries	6310						

Expenses	Acct#	1 Prior Year Budget	2 Prior Year Actual	3 Over (under)	4 Adjust- ments Incr. (Decr.)	5 New Annual Budget	6 Adjust- ments By HUD
9. Office Exp.	6311						
10. Misc. Adm. Exp.	6390						
11.							
12.							
13.							
14.							
15. Fuel	6420						
16. Electricity	6450						
17. Water & Sewer	6451						
18. Veh. & Equip. Oper. Exp.	6441						
19. Janitor's Payroll	6430						
20. Janitor's Supplies	6431						
21. Exterminating	6462						
22. Rubbish Removal	6470						
23. Parking Area Exp.	6480						
24.							
25.							
26.							

MANAGEMENT AND BUDGET

Expenses	Acct#	1 Prior Year Budget	2 Prior Year Actual	3 Over (under)	4 Adjust- ments Incr. (Decr.)	5 New Annual Budget	6 Adjust- ments By HUD
27. Grounds Main- tenance	6520						
28. Painting & Deco- rating	6560						
29. Struc- tural Re- pairs	6540						
30. Heating & Air Cond. Main- tenance	6510						
31. Plumbing Main- tenance	6511						
32. Electri- cal Main- tenance	6512						
33. Elevator Main- tenance	6550						
34. Pool Main- tenance	6521						
35. Main- tenance Sup- plies	6515						
36. Main- tenance & Pay- roll	6585						

Expenses	Acct#	1 Prior Year Budget	2 Prior Year Actual	3 Over (under)	4 Adjust- ments Incr. (Decr.)	5 New Annual Budget	6 Adjust- ments By HUD
37. Mis. Main- tenance	6590						
38.							
39. Real Es- state Taxes	6710						
40. Employ- er's Payroll Taxes	6711						
41. Mis. Taxes	6719						
42. Property & Lia- bility Insur.	6720						
43. Work- men's Comp.	6721						
44. Fidelity Bonds	6723						
45. Misc. Insur.	6729						
46.							
47.							
48.							
49. Ground Rent	6815						
50. Mortgage Insur. Premium	6850						
51. Mortgage In- terest	6820						

Expenses	Acct#	1 Prior Year Budget	2 Prior Year Actual	3 Over (under)	4 Adjust- ments Incr. (Decr.)	5 New Annual Budget	6 Adjust- ments By HUD
52. Mortgage Princi- pal	2320						
53. Replace- ment Re- serve	1320						
54. General Oper- ating Re- serve	1365						
55. Painting Re- serve	1330						
56. Project Equip- ment Purch.	1470						
57. Capital Improve- ments	1400						
TOTAL EXPENSE							

Column #4 reflects necessary or desirable increases
and decreases over prior year's budget (col.#1) to
arrive at New Annual Budget (Col. #5).
Carrying Charges and other budgeted income (line
#68) must at least equal the total expenses on

146

line #58. Lines 52-57 provide for capital contribution by members, in excess of their down payments, and should be entered in the books through
Account #3241 (Paid-in Surplus).

Surcharges received from occupants in Section 221(d)
(3) and Section 236 cases are not budget items
and should not be reflected in any of the columns
in Line 59 nor in the Schedule of Carrying Charges,
but should be reflected in a separate Schedule.
Additional instructions for the preparation of
this form are contained in HUD handbook HM 4371.2,
the Uniform System of Accounts for Cooperative
Housing Corporations.

Expenses	Acct#	1 Prior Year Budget	2 Prior Year Actual	3 Over (under)	4 Adjust ments Incr. (Decr.)	5 New Annual Budget	6 Adjust ments By HUD
59.Carrying Charges	5110						
60.Late Charges	5910	xxxx	xxxx	xxxx	xxxx	xxxx	xxxx
61.Interest Income	5410						
62.							
63.							
64.							
65.							
66.							
67.							
68.TOTAL INCOME							
69.TOTAL EXPENSE (line 58)							
70.Income over (Under) Expense							

MANAGEMENT AND BUDGET

STATUS OF FUNDED RESERVES

Acct.#	Required to Date	Actual on Deposit	Excess (Deficiency)	
A. Replace-ment Re-service	1320			Provision for Repayment of Any De-ficiences
B. Gen. Opr. Re-serve	1365			Should be Included in Lines 53, 54,
C. Painting Re-serve	3730			and 55.
D.				
E.				
F.				

SCHEDULE OF CARRYING CHARGES

Description of Unit	# of Units of this type	MON. CARRY. CHGS. Prior Yr. New Yr.		ANNUAL CARRY. CHGS. Prior Yr. New Yr.	
TOTAL					

Unless otherwise indicated it is assumed that all utilities, maintenance and replacements are provided by the cooperative and are included in the above carrying charges. If any, of these items are paid for directly by the member check below. (Specify any other items not listed)

Utilities /‾/   Fuel /‾/   Electricity /‾/   Water_____

Replace. /‾/ Range /‾/ Refrig. /‾/ Air Cond. /‾/ Garb. Disp.____

Main. /‾/   Range /‾/ Refrig. /‾/ Air Cond. /‾/ Garg. Disp.___

Explanatory comments, including management agents' opinion
as to adequacy of proposed new budget:

Prepared By,   Approved:

_____   _____
Managing Agent   Title_____
                                             (On Behalf of Condo.)
Date_____   Date_____

Approved: Approved as indicated in
                                      column 6:

_____   _____
(Signature and Title of   (Signature and Title of
 Authorized Official)   Authorized Official)

Date_____   _____

IX. Financing

IX. Financing

A condominium is financed in two phases. The developer finances construction through an overall or "blanket" mortgage. Then the potential owners assume individual mortgages on the separate units after the developer has fulfilled certain requirements. The buyers form an Association of Apartment Owners, and elect a board of directors to administer the common elements, which they now own jointly.

FHA rules governing financing of the first blanket mortgage are designed to protect both the lending institutions and future buyers.

The blanket mortgage is usually for a certain percent of the building costs of each unit. Under FHA rules, this means no more than 90% of its replacement value. A developer must show that he has or will have clear title to the land on which

the condominium will be built and prove his assets
will cover the liability, as in any other credit
transaction.

Prospective buyers are protected by the
provision that no part of their down payment can
be used until over 80% of the development is sold.
FHA codes further stipulate that the blanket
mortgage must be paid off when the project is
completed. Before title can be conveyed to the
purchasers, the developer must guarantee it to be
free and clear of liens. If, for any reason, the
project isn't completed, the purchaser is entitled
to the return of his down payment.

Because of the demand for this type of housing,
lenders are receptive to the needs of condominium
developers, provided they can show adequate assets
and/or a good track record in construction or
other sound business ventures. If the lender has
had previous experience with condominium loans,
his advice on location, style and other matters
can be of assistance to a developer who is new to
the field.

Since their interests, like those of the
developer, lie in potential successful sales
volume, financers of blanket mortgages have to
be assured that the project will attract buyers.
They sometimes insist that if all units aren't

sold, rental arrangements can be made for them
until full occupancy is a reality.

Lenders also check on the proposed sales
campaign for the development. They will want to
know whether or not it incorporates and will
fully publicize all the amenities available to
buyers. This is particularly important in areas
where other successful condominiums haven't been
established and there may be possible buyer
resistance toward a project which is yet to be
built.

It can't be emphasized too much that all
legal hurdles must have been cleared before
approaching a lender. The cost of a first class
real estate attorney who is well acquainted with
the regulations of comdominium building in any
given locality should be considered as insurance
for successful completion. Advice on the
statutorial "lay of the land" in the area of a
proposed condominium is as important as knowing
the physical assets of the property if the builder
expects to get his financing approved with a
minimum of delays.

FINANCING

REGULATORY AGREEMENT*

(For use by condominiums under Section 221(i), 234 and 235)

AGREEMENT dated this   day of
      , 19   , by and between   **
(hereinafter called the Association) whose address
is   party
of the first part, and   , as
Federal Housing Commission (hereinafter called the
Commissioner) acting pursuant to authority granted
him by the National Housing Act, as amended, (hereinafter referred to as the Act) party of the second
part.

WHEREAS, the Association has the responsibility
for administering the
Condominium and desires to aid members in obtaining
financing for the purchase of family units in the
condominium; and

WHEREAS, mortgagees may be unwilling to lend
sums to the members of the Association without
FHA mortgage insurance; and

WHEREAS, the Commissioner is unwilling to
endorse notes for mortgage insurance pursuant to
Section 234 of Title II of the Act unless and
until the Association shall be entering into the
covenants and agreements set forth below, consent
to be regulated and restricted by the Commissioner
as provided in the Act:

NOW, THEREFORE, in consideration of One Dollar
($1.00) in hand paid, and other good and valuable

---

*To be attached to the recorded Plan of Apartment
Ownership and to be executed and dated as of the date of
recordation.

**Insert name of Association of Owners as designated
in the By-Laws of the Condominium, or the name of the
Corporation, if the Association is incorporated.

considerations by each party to the other, the receipt of which is hereby acknowledged, and in order to induce the Commissioner to endorse for mortgage insurance the notes secured by mortgages covering family units in the condominium, and in order that the Association may be regulated and restricted by the Commissioner as provided for in the Act and the applicable Regulations, the parties hereto agree as follows: that whenever a Contract of Mortgage Insurance for a mortgage covering a family unit in the condominium is in effect, or during any period of time as the Commissioner shall be the owner, holder, or re-insurer of any mortgage covering a family unit in the condominium, or during any time the Commissioner is the owner of a family unit in the condominium or is obligated to insure a mortgage covering any family unit in the condo-minium:

1. The Association shall establish and maintain reserve fund for replacements by the allocation and payment monthly to such reserve fund an amount to be designated from time to time by the Commissioner. Such fund shall be deposited in a special account with a safe and responsible depository approved by the Commissioner and may be in the form of a cash deposit or invested in obligations of, or fully guaranteed as to principal by, the United States of America. The reserve fund is for the purpose of effect-ing replacements of structural elements and mechanical equipment of the condominium and for such other purposes as may be agreed to in writing by the Commissioner. Disbursements from such fund may be made only after receiving the consent in writing of the Commissioner.

2. The Association shall establish and maintain a general operating reserve by allocation and payment thereto monthly of a sum equivalent to not less than 3 percent of the monthly assessments chargeable to the owners of family units in the condominium pursuant to the By-Laws. Upon accrual in said General Operating

Reserve Account of an amount equal to 15 percent
of the current annual amount of assessments
chargeable to the owners of family units in the
condominium pursuant to the By-Laws, the rate
of such monthly allocations may, by appropriate
action of the Association, be reduced from 3
percent to 2 percent provided, however, that
in the event withdrawals from such account
reduce it below said 15 percent accrual, the
rate of such monthly deposits shall immediately
be restored to 3 percent; at any time thereafter
upon accrual in said General Operating Reserve
Account of an amount equal to 25 percent of the
current annual amount of assessments chargeable
to the owners of family units in the condominium
pursuant to the By-Laws, such monthly deposits
may, by appropriate action of the Association,
be discontinued and no further deposits need
be made into such General Operating Reserve so
long as said 25 percent level is maintained
and provided, further, that upon reduction of
such reserve below said 25 percent level,
monthly deposits shall forthwith be made at
the 3 percent rate until the 25 percent level
is restored. This reserve shall remain in a
special account and may be in the form of cash
deposit or invested in obligations of, or fully
guaranteed as to principal by, the United States
of America, and shall at all times be under the
control of the Association. This cumulative
reserve is intended to provide a measure of
financial stability during periods of special
stress and may be used to meet deficiencies
from time to time as a result of delinquent
payments of assessments by owners of family
units in the condominium and other contingencies
Disbursements totalling in excess of 20 percent
of the total balance in the reserve as of the
close of the preceding annual period may not
be made during any annual period without the
consent of the Commissioner. Reimbursements
shall be made to the account upon payment of
the delinquencies for which funds were with-
drawn from the reserve.

3. The Association will not employ a management

agent for the buildings nor enter into a
management contract nor undertake "self-
management" unless the Commissioner has approved
in writing the proposed management agent, form
of management contract or other management
arrangement.

4. The Association shall not without prior approval
    of the Commissioner, given in writing, remodel,
    reconstruct, demolish or subtract from the
    premises constituting the condominium.

5. The Association shall not without prior
    approval of the Commissioner given in writing:

    (a) amend or change the Plan of Apartment
        Ownership or the By-Laws of the
        Associatoin;
    (b) fail to establish and maintain the Fund
        for Replacements and general operating
        reserve as set forth herein;
    (c) fail to provide for the management of
        the condominium in a manner approved by
        the Commissioner;
    (d) fail to keep in full force and effect
        an elevator contract satisfactory to the
        FHA covering the maintenance and replace-
        ment of parts of any elevator or related
        equipment, or, if such contract shall be
        allowed to expire, then fail to accrue
        an additional sum in such amount as shall
        be designated by the Commissioner to be
        sufficient to allow for deferred and
        future replacements as part of the
        annual Reserve for Replacement Fund
        collected by the Association so as to
        insure that Funds will be available for
        replacement of elevator parts and related
        equipment.

6. The Association shall maintain the common areas
    and facilities, and each owner of a family unit
    shall maintain the family unit, in good repair
    and in such condition as will preserve the
    health and safety of the members.

FINANCING

7. The books, contracts, records, documents and papers of the Association and all of the property of the condominium shall be subject to inspection and examination by the Commissioner or his duly authorized agent at all reasonable times. The Association shall file with the Commissioner the following reports verified by the signature of such officers of the Association as may be designated and in such form as may be prescribed by the Commissioner:

   (a) monthly operating reports, when required by the Commissioner;
   (b) annual financial reports prepared by a certified public accountant or other person acceptable to the Commissioner within sixty days after the end of each fiscal year;
   (c) specific answers to questions upon which information is desired from time to time relative to the operation and condition of the property;
   (d) copies of minutes of all owners' meetings certified to by the secretary of the Association within thirty days after such meetings, and when required by the Commissioner, copies of minutes of directors' meetings.

8. The Association shall establish and collect from owners of family units monthly assessments pursuant to the conditions set forth herein. Monthly assessments charged to owners during the initial occupancy period shall be made by the Association in accordance with a schedule of charges filed with and approved in writing by the Commissioner prior to the opening of the project for occupancy. Such assessment shall be in an amount sufficient to meet the FHA estimate of management expense, operating expense, and maintenance expense, reserves, and all other expenses of the Association. Subsequent to the initial occupancy period, assessments made by the Association for its accommodations shall be in accordance with a

schedule filed with and approved in writing
by the Commissioner and shall be in amounts
sufficient to meet the Association's estimate
of expenses set forth in an operating budget
which shall be prepared and submitted to
the FHA sixty days prior to the beginning
of each fiscal year. The operating budget
shall set forth the anticipated income of the
Association and a sufficiently detailed estimate of expenses which will include separate
estimates for administration expense, operating expense, maintenance expense, utilities,
hazard insurance, replacement reserve and
operating reserve. Such assessments shall not
be changed except with the written approval of
the Commissioner. The Association agrees that
if at any time the owner of a family unit fails
to pay his monthly assessment as provided in
the By-Laws, the Association will, upon
direction of the Commissioner, initiate
necessary legal action to collect the asess-
ment.

9. Upon a violation of any of the above provisions
   of this Agreement by the Association, or by
   any owner of a family unit, or upon the failure
   of the Association to abide by and carry out
   the provisions of the Plan of Apartment Ownership and the By-Laws, the Commissioner may
   give written notice thereof to the Association
   or to the owner of a family unit, by registered
   or certified mail. If such violation is not
   corrected to the satisfaction of the Commissioner
   within 15 days after the date such notice is
   mailed, or within such additional period of
   time as is set forth in the notice, without
   further notice the Commissioner may declare
   a default under this Agreement and upon such
   default the Commissioner may:

   (a) In the case of a default by the owner
       of a family unit:
       (i) If the Commissioner holds the note
           of the defaulting owner - declare
           the whole of said indebtedness due

       and payable and then proceed with
       the foreclosure of the mortgage;

(ii) If said note is held by an FHA-
insured mortgagee - notify the
mortgagee of such default, and the
mortgagee, with the prior written
consent of the Commissioner, may
declare the whole indebtedness due,
and thereupon proceed with the
foreclosure of the mortgage, or
assign the note and mortgage to
the Commissioner as provided in
the Regulations.

(b) In the case of a default by the Association or by the owner of a family unit:
    Apply to any court, State or Federal,
for specific performance of this
Agreement, for an injunction against
any violation of the Agreement, or
for such other relief as may be
appropriate, since the injury to the
Commissioner arising from a default
under any of the terms of this
Agreement would be irreparable and
the amount of damage would be
difficult to ascertain.

10. The covenants and agreements herein set out shall
be deemed to run with the land and the property
described in the Plan of Apartment Ownership,
and to bind all owners of family units, present
and future.

11. As used in this Agreement the term:

(a) "Mortgage" shall include "Deed of Trust";
(b) "Note" shall include "Bond";
(c) "Mortgagee" shall include the "Beneficiary"
under Mortgage or Deed of Trust however
designated;
(d) "Default" means a default declared by
the Commissioner when a violation of
this Agreement is not corrected to his
satisfaction within the time allowed by
this Agreement or such further time as

may be allowed by the Commissioner after written notice;

(e) "Plan of Apartment Ownership" shall include all legal documents, deeds, By-Laws, plans and specifications, required by the laws of the jurisdiction to establish condominium ownership.

(The use of the plural shall include the singular; the singular the plural; and the use of any gender shall be deemed to include all genders.)

12. This instrument shall bind, and the benefits shall inure to, the respective parties hereto, their legal representatives, executors, administrators, successors in office or interest, and assigns.

13. The invalidity of any clause, part or provision of this agreement shall not affect the validity of the remaining portions thereof.

14. The Association agrees and assumes the obligation to have this Agreement recorded in the appropriate land records in the jurisdiction in which the real property herein described is situated; and in the event of failure to do so, it is agreed that the Commissioner may have the same recorded at the expense of the Association.

15. It is specifically agreed between the parties hereto that the breach of any of the terms of this Agreement by the Association or by an owner of a family unit will substantially damage and injure the Commissioner in the proper performance of his duties under the provisions of the Act, and will impede and injure the proper operations intended under such Act; that such damage will be irrespective of and in addition to any damage to the security of the mortgaged premises or to any financial damage the Commissioner may suffer as insurer; that, except for the agreements herein contained, the Commissioner would not issue and would not

FINANCING

be authorized to issue a Contract of Mortgage
Insurance, and that mortgagees may not be
willing to lend sums of money to owners of
the family units on the security of mortgages
covering such units, unless the same were
insured by the Commissioner.

IN WITNESS WHEREOF the parties hereto have duly
executed this Agreement the day and year first
above written.

ASSOCIATION OF OWNERS OF   CONDOMINIUM

WITNESS:

_____   _____(SEAL)

_____   _____(SEAL)

FEDERAL HOUSING COMMISSIONER

_____   _____
                                    (Authorized Agent)

_____

ACKNOWLEDGMENT OF ASSOCIATION OF OWNERS
OF _____ CONDOMINIUM
(In accordance with the form in State
where property is located)

X. Adjoining Condominiums And Home Owner Associations

X. Adjoining Condominiums And Home Owner Associations

The basic meaning of the word condominium is "owning together". In the modern sense this refers particularly to common elements shared by individual owners. The idea of a group of people living in separate homes but sharing other areas is realized in both adjoining condominiums and home owner associations.

In the case of adjoining condominiums, a developer may wish to build a series of condominiums and to complete and sell each before starting another None of the units, taken alone, would support facilities such as a community recreation center, but when the project is finished, the owners could afford to finance commonly-owned "off-site" areas. The developer may use the proposed amenities as a selling point for buyers, although they won't be completed when some of the owners take possesion of their individual units.

ADJOINING CONDOS & HOME OWNER ASSOC.

Although such common areas will not be
completed when the first, or even the second unit
is sold out, the contemplated facilities and the
land on which they are to be located must be included in the Master Deed. If there will be 100
units, each owner must begin paying his 1/100th
share of "off-site" expenses, even though he can't
enjoy them yet. When the condominium is finished,
the developer is liable for the share of common
costs in unsold units until he finds a buyer.

After all the individual units are sold, the
former "off-site" facility becomes part of the
condominium property, as provided for in the
Master Deed, and becomes subject to all rules and
regulations of the Apartment Owners Association.

HOME OWNER ASSOCIATIONS

A home owners association is created by
residents of a community with open land areas which
they want to convert into commonly held property,
usually for recreational purposes. Such an association allows a neighborhood to keep its tradition
of detached houses while still enjoying facilities
which would be too expensive for individual owners
to maintain.

The Association first incorporates itself as
a non-profit corporation and establishes legal
title to the property. Following this, the pro-

cedure is the same as that in organizing a conventional condominium, except that in this case the owners create their own condominium rather than a developer, or middleman, constructing a project with both private units and common facilities which he then offers for ownership.

Members of a non-profit home owners association bind themselves by the same rules that govern other jointly owned ventures. The right to use the common facilities and limitations on such use is defined in the articles of incorporation. The board of directors of the association is responsible for operating and maintaining the common property within the limits set by the assessments on members, and membership is automatically transferred upon sale of an individual home.

The home owners association concept offers a chance for individuals who don't want to leave their neighborhood to participate in condominium benefits. They can combine the advantages of joint common property ownership with the investments already made in personal relationships and their individual homes without giving up a chance to enjoy their present life style. Rather than having to move, they improve the value of their community.

XI. Condominiums For Low Income Households

XI. Condominiums For Low Income Households

The condominium concept when applied to low-income households provides an opportunity for such a family to acquire a home. Although developers can't offer the characteristic suburban single-family dwelling to people in crowded urban areas, apartment ownership is now possible.

People who have always paid rent because they couldn't afford property in the city and could even less afford to move away from it can now consider the advantages of permanent occupancy, tax breaks, pride of ownership and possible resale at a profit. The latter, of course, depends on how the property has been maintained.

The 1968 Housing and Urban Development Act provided for mortgage loans below the market and financial breaks to institutions and municipalities to stimulate a program designed to help the poor

to help themselves. . .not to the public treasury
but to self-respecting home ownership.

The plan was not meant to be a panacea and
eliminate all inner-city eyesores overnight, but
was meant to make a start in the right direction.
The basic idea was that when existing buildings are
converted into condominiums, former renters become
owners, with equity in their units. Money formerly
spent on rent, now put into mortgage payments instead,
would allow the occupants to build up an equity and
subsequently, pride of ownership. Pride of ownership would, in turn, lead to better care of the
property and a gradual increase in its value.

It takes time to change attitudes and the HUD
program is still too new to the housing scene to be
assessed. Administration of the law varies in
different areas and progress has been further hampered by unworkable rules and confusing paperwork,
both bugaboos to be expected in getting a compli-
cated new program to operate efficiently.

One of the stumbling blocks concerns management. One faction at the administrative level
believes the people concerned are incapable of
management and it should be kept out of their hands.
Another group believes just as strongly that the
hoped-for pride of ownership will never develop
without participation in management decisions by
the people involved. This participation is, by

its nature, a cornerstone of the condominium
philosophy.

Allowing owners, who have developed and improved
their property, to keep the profits of sales is also
disputed. In developments where this was allowed,
however, resale values were three times as high as
where they weren't.

Since these projects are subsidized by the
government, either through direct rent subsidies
to individuals and/or sites and services provided,
anything that would be detrimental to the agency
in charge is effectively suppressed. This stifles
progress in working out problems caused by hasty
planning and perpetuates the errors.

If and when these problems can be solved,
condominium ownership by low income families can
be the start of a needed development, both in
human resources and restructuring the value of
blighted areas.

Conclusion

Conclusion

There have been at least as many condominium failures as there have been successes. Most of the failures were caused by lack of adherence to one or more of the basic (but important) general principles set forth in this book. Conversely, strict attention to these guidelines can ensure ultimate success.

Condominiums are now a major fact of life in our real estate world. Where unnatural restrictions and moratoriums have been legislated, they are gradually being lifted to fulfill the dire housing needs of American society. So, undoubtedly, you will, at one time or another, seriously consider this form of real estate investment for yourself. It is sincerely hoped that this book will be used as it was intended: as a sourcebook and referential guide through the labrynth of confusion and red-tape - - - to peace of mind and financial reward.

Bibliography

ALI-ABA Course of Study: *Real Estate Condominiums*.
ALI-ABA Course of Study, Real Estate Condo-
miniums, Friday, Sept. 20, and Sept. 21, 1974,
Charlottesville, Va. American Law Institute,
American Bar Association, Committee on
Continuing Professional Education, 1974.

Arnold, Alvin L. *Developing A Condominium*: Feasibility,
Financing and Marketing; Special Report.
Boston, Warren, Gorham, & Lamont, 1973.

Associated Homebuilders of the Greater Eastery.
The Condominium Development and Conversion Handbook.
Berkeley, California, 1973.

Brooks, Patricia K. *How To Buy A Condominium*. Boston,
G.K. Hall, 1977.

Butcher, Lee. *The Condominium Book*. Princeton, N.J.,
Dow Jones Books, 1975.

Calevas, Harry Powell. *Condominium Management Handbook*.
Boca Raton, Fla., Evinland, 1977.

Christison, D.B. *Budget Preparation Guide For Condominium
Homeowner Associations*. San Jose, Ca., Executive
Council of Homeowners, 1975.

Clurman, David. *Condominums and Cooperatives*. New York,
Wiley-Interscience, 1970.

Community Management Cooperation. *Financial Management of Condominium and Homeowners Association.* Washington, Urban Land Institute, 1975.

Condominium: How To Put Together A New Condominium Law, Regulations, and Forms. Los Angeles, California Real Estate Association, 1971.

Condominium Development. New York, Practicing Law Institute, 1969.

Condominium Development, 2d. New York, Practicing Law Institute, 1972.

Cooperatives and Condominiums. New York, Practicing Law Institute, 1969.

Development and Financing of Condominiums. New York, Practicing Law Institute, 1973.

Dombal, Robert W. *Residential Condominiums.* Chicago, American Institute of Real Estate Appraisers of the National Association of Realtors, 1976.

Epstein, Lisa. *Condominiums:* Financial and Legal Aspects. Sacramento, California State Library, Law Library, 1972.

Gardner, C.D. *The Condominium Handbook.* Berkeley, Associated Home Builders of the Greater Eastery, 1970.

Government Regulation of Condominiums. New York, Practicing Law Institute, 1974.

Gray, Genevieve S. *Condominiums:* How to Buy, Sell and Live in Them. New York, Funk & Wagnalls, 1975.

Grezzo, Anthony D. *Condominiums:* Their Development and Management. Washington, Office of Internal Affairs, Dept. of Housing and Urban Development, 1972.

Gwinuf, Thomas. *Residential Condominiums.* San Diego, San Diego State University Library, 1978.

Hiffaka, William H. *Factors Contributing to the Success or Failure of Residential Condominium Developments;* In San Diego County, California. San Diego, Calif., Bureau of Business and Economic Research, School of Business Administration,

San Diego State University, 1972.

How to List and Sell Condominium Homes. Los Angeles,
    Calif. Association of Realtors, 1975.

Johnson, Donald. *The Condominium Concept.* Hayward,
    Associated Building Industry of Northern
    Calif., 1974.

Kehoe, Patrick E. *Cooperatives and Condominiums.* Dobbs
    Ferry, New York, Oceana Publications, 1974.

National Association of Attorneys General.
    Committee on the Office of Attorney General.
    Land and Condominium Sales Regulation. Raleigh,
    N.C. The Committee, 1975.

Norcross, Carl. *Townhouses & Condominiums:* Residents
    Likes and Dislikes. Washington, Urban Land
    Institute, 1973.

Rohan, Patrick J. *Home Owner Associations and Planned
    Unit Developments Law and Practice.* New York,
    M. Bender, 1977.

Rothenberg, Henry H. *What You Should Know About
    Condominiums.* Radnor, Pa., Chilton Book Co.,
    1974.

Scele, Bernard D. *Transtationary Dwelling Condominium
    Development.* Detroit, 1973.

Sheldon, Roy. *Know the Ins and Outs of Condominium
    Buying.* New York I.E. Jerico, N.Y., Exposition
    Press, 1973.

Szego, George C. *Cost-Reducing Condominium Systems for
    Low-Cost Homes.* Arlington, Va., 1968.

The Law and Condominium Development. Halifax, Faculty
    of Law Dalousie University, 1973.

The Practical Lawyer's Manual of Modern Real Estate Practices.
    Philadelphia, Joint Committee on Continuing
    Legal Education of the American Institute and
    the American Bar Association, 1969.

Thompson, Elisabeth Kendall. *Apartments, Townhouses,
    and Condominiums.* New York, McGraw Hill, 1975.

Tymon, Dorothy. *The Condominium.* New York, Avon, 1976

Urban Land Institute. *Managing a Successful Community Association.* Washington, published jointly by the Urban Land Institute and the Community Associations Institute, 1974.

Vogts, Alfred. *How To Buy a Condominium.* Miami, Hurricane House, 1969.

Weisman, Joshua. *The Condominium Law.* Jerusalem, Institute for Legislative Research and Comparative Law, 1970.

INDEX

About The Author

Over the past 25 years, Adam Starchild has been the author of over two dozen books, and hundreds of magazine articles, primarily on business and finance. His articles have appeared in a wide range of publications around the world -- including Business Credit, Euromoney, Finance, The Financial Planner, International Living, Offshore Financial Review, Reason, Tax Planning International, The Bull & Bear, Trust & Estates, and many more.

Now semi-retired, he was the president of an international consulting group specializing in banking, finance and the development of new businesses, and director of a trust company.

Although this formidable testimony to expertise in his field, plus his current preoccupation with other books-in-progress, would not seem to leave time for a well-rounded existence, Starchild has won two Presidential Sports Awards and written several cookbooks, and is currently involved in a number of personal charitable projects. His website is at http://www.adamstarchild.com

Printed in the United States
62999LVS00005B/32